USING THE

NATIONAL GIFTED EDUCATION STANDARDS

FOR PREK-12

PROFESSIONAL DEVELOPMENT

USING THE
NATIONAL GIFTED EDUCATION STANDARDS
FOR PreK–12
PROFESSIONAL DEVELOPMENT

MARGIE KITANO   DIANE MONTGOMERY   JOYCE VANTASSEL-BASKA   SUSAN K. JOHNSEN

A JOINT PUBLICATION
NATIONAL ASSOCIATION FOR GIFTED CHILDREN
COUNCIL FOR EXCEPTIONAL CHILDREN
THE ASSOCIATION FOR THE GIFTED

CORWIN PRESS
A SAGE Company
Thousand Oaks, CA 91320

For information:

Corwin Press
A SAGE Company
2455 Teller Road
Thousand Oaks, California 91320
www.corwinpress.com

SAGE Ltd.
1 Oliver's Yard
55 City Road
London EC1Y 1SP
United Kingdom

SAGE India Pvt. Ltd.
B 1/I 1 Mohan Cooperative Industrial Area
Mathura Road, New Delhi 110 044
India

SAGE Asia-Pacific Pte. Ltd.
33 Pekin Street #02-01
Far East Square
Singapore 048763

Printed in the United States of America.

A catalog record of this book is available from the Library of Congress.

ISBN 978-1-4129-6522-4 (cloth)
ISBN 978-1-4129-6523-1 (pbk.)

This book is printed on acid-free paper.

08   09   10   11   12   10   9   8   7   6   5   4   3   2   1

Acquisitions Editor:	David Chao
Editorial Assistant:	Mary Dang
Production Editor:	Libby Larson
Copy Editor:	Linda Gray
Typesetter:	C&M Digitals (P) Ltd.
Proofreader:	Jenifer Kooiman
Indexer:	Marilyn Augst
Cover Designer:	Scott Van Atta
Graphic Designer:	Karine Hovsepian

Contents

Appendixes

Foreword

James J. Gallagher, PhD
University of North Carolina at Chapel Hill

I greatly appreciate the opportunity to comment on this significant document, which will move forward the gifted education profession. This is a companion book to *Using the National Gifted Education Standards for University Teacher Preparation Programs*. They are both products of four years of effort by working groups from the National Association for Gifted Children (NAGC) and The Association for the Gifted (TAG).

The newly adopted standards for university personnel preparation alone are not sufficient to reach the goal of quality instruction for gifted learners in our schools, partly because not every college of education offers course work in gifted education but also because current personnel preparation programs in elementary and secondary education typically offer scant mention of this topic even though general education teachers will have the major responsibility in educating our gifted and talented youth. Currently, teachers who wish to learn more about how to work with advanced learners must attend workshops or convention programs or seek written material on the topic.

It was extremely important therefore that the NAGC and TAG working group produce guides devoted to reaching not only teachers entering the profession but also those who have been on the firing line for many years without specific instruction or standards. Four members of the working group—Margie Kitano, Diane Montgomery, Joyce VanTassel-Baska, and Susan Johnsen—have produced this book focusing on how school systems and state departments of education can develop a systematic program of in-service training in this field. Their stated purpose was "to assist PreK–12 program leaders in gifted education identify needed knowledge and skills for professional development based on national standards for teachers of students with gifts and talents."

The 10 key standards include mastering knowledge about students with gifts and talents, the special instructional strategies and planning needed for such students and the assessment of such special efforts. The standards themselves are presented in Chapter 2 by Johnsen. Kitano produces a necessary chapter (Chapter 9) on diversity, taking each of the 10 standards and showing specifically how they relate to students of diversity who have special gifts and talents. The continued underrepresentation of minority groups in programs for children with gifts and talents is warning enough of how we have overlooked much potential talent.

VanTassel-Baska presents a template for in-service training program leaders to follow when developing a personnel preparation plan (Chapter 6), and Montgomery presents a variety of strategies to facilitate teacher learning, including mentoring or shadowing other teachers, teacher-led seminars, team teaching, classroom coaching, collaborative curriculum planning, and action research projects (Chapter 7) . There are also some innovative ways of assessing these strategies including observation scales and needs assessment devices.

We in this field are in debt to the professionals who devoted the time and effort necessary to move our field forward in this dramatic and specific way and to NAGC and TAG for facilitating this effort. It remains for the rest of us to ensure that such progress becomes a living and breathing part of the future of educating students with gifts and talents.

Acknowledgments

While the authors are responsible for the content, the guidebook resulted from the combined efforts of numerous colleagues who contributed to the standards' development and encouraged our efforts to apply them to professional practice in PreK–12 schools: Nancy Green and Jane Clarenbach at the National Association for Gifted Children; Richard Mainzer, Kathlene Shank, Mary Ruth Coleman, and the Knowledge and Skills Subcommittee at the Council for Exceptional Children; the Boards of the National Association for Gifted Children and The Association for the Gifted; and standards task force members Ann Robinson, Karen Rogers, and Richard Olenchak. We especially appreciate the school district and state-level teachers and administrators who shared their visions of evidence-supported professional development and whose examples inspired our work.

About the Authors

Margie Kitano, PhD, serves as Associate Dean of the College of Education and Professor of Special Education at San Diego State University (SDSU). She codeveloped and works with the San Diego Unified School District on a collaborative certificate in gifted education. The program combines current theory and research with best practices to support services to gifted students, with special attention to underrepresented populations. Her current research and publications focus on improving services to culturally and linguistically diverse gifted learners.

Diane Montgomery, PhD, is Professor of Educational Psychology at Oklahoma State University in the College of Education where she coordinates graduate programs in gifted education. Her areas of expertise and research include creativity, transpersonal psychology, Native American Indian education, gifted and talented education, and teacher development. She has held positions on several editorial boards and boards of directors of national professional organizations, including The Association for the Gifted, a division of the Council for Exceptional Children and American Council on Rural Special Education.

Joyce VanTassel-Baska, EdD, is the Jody and Layton Smith Professor of Education and Executive Director of the Center for Gifted Education at The College of William and Mary in Virginia, where she has developed a graduate program and a research and development center in gifted education. Formerly, she initiated and directed the Center for Talent Development at Northwestern University. She is a past president of The Association for the Gifted of the Council for Exceptional Children and of the Northwestern University Chapter of Phi Delta Kappa. She is past president of the National Association for Gifted Children. During her tenure as NAGC president, she oversaw the adoption of the new NCATE standards for gifted education and organized and chaired the National Leadership Conference on Promising and Low-Income Learners. She has published widely, including 22 books and over 500 refereed journal articles, book chapters, and scholarly reports. Recent books include *Alternative Assessment With Gifted and Talented Students* (2008) and *Serving Gifted Learners Beyond the Traditional Classroom* (2007). Also, she has received numerous awards for her work, including the National Association for Gifted Children's Early Leader Award in 1986, the State Council of Higher Education in Virginia Outstanding Faculty Award in 1993, the Phi Beta Kappa faculty award in 1995, the National Association for Gifted Children Distinguished Scholar Award in 1997, and the President's Award, World Council on Gifted and Talented Education in 2005. She has received awards from five states—Ohio, Virginia, Colorado, South Carolina, and Illinois—for her contribution to the field of gifted education in those states.

Susan K. Johnsen, PhD, is professor in the Department of Educational Psychology at Baylor University. She directs the PhD program and programs related to gifted and talented education. She has written more than 150 articles, monographs, technical reports, and books related to gifted education. She is a frequent presenter at international, national, and state conferences. She is editor of *Gifted Child Today* and serves on the boards of *Gifted Child Quarterly, Journal for the Education of the Gifted*, and *Roeper Review.* She is the author of *Identifying Gifted Students: A Practical Guide,* coauthor of the Independent Study program and coauthor of three tests used in identifying gifted students: Test of Mathematical Abilities for Gifted Students (TOMAGS), Test of Nonverbal Intelligence (TONI-3), and Screening Assessment for Gifted Students (SAGES-2). She is president of The Association for the Gifted, Council for Exceptional Children and past president of the Texas Association for Gifted and Talented.

Introduction

Professional development for teachers in gifted education can take many forms, including participation in district-sponsored workshops and courses, university courses, professional conferences, independent study, and presentations by consultants and other external parties. Critical to all forms of professional development is determining appropriate objectives and assessing impact on teachers and their students. This guide was developed to assist PreK–12 program leaders in gifted education identify needed knowledge and skills for professional development based on national standards for teachers of students with gifts and talents. Working collaboratively over a four-year period, representatives from The Association for the Gifted (CEC-TAG) and the National Association for Gifted Children (NAGC) developed a set of standards that define essential knowledge and skills for effective teaching of gifted and talented students based on the research.

The guidebook shares the standards, summarizes supporting research, and describes how the standards can be used to plan professional development in gifted education. Included are suggestions for identifying needs, aligning various sets of standards to develop objectives, generating professional development plans and activities, considering the needs of culturally diverse gifted learners, and assessing outcomes. It also provides an exemplary district-level professional development program that may be used as a model. The appendixes provide sample needs and outcome assessment instruments and planning forms.

Margie Kitano, Diane Montgomery,
Joyce VanTassel-Baska, and Susan K. Johnsen

National Standards for Preparation of Teachers of the Gifted

History and Implications for PreK–12 Schools

Margie Kitano

What are the national standards for preparation of teachers of the gifted? How do we know they are valid? What are their implications for PreK–12 teachers, schools, and districts?

NATIONAL STANDARDS AND PREK–12 SCHOOLS

An unprecedented, multiyear collaboration of the Council for Exceptional Children's The Association for the Gifted (TAG) and the National Association for Gifted Children (NAGC) resulted in new standards for entry-level teachers of the gifted, approved in the fall of 2006. The standards, validated by professional literature in the field, were designed for the accreditation of university preparation programs in gifted education through the National Council for Accreditation of Teacher

Education (NCATE). These standards identify what beginning teachers of the gifted should know and be able to do.

Only a small number of universities offer programs that prepare teachers specifically for working with gifted and talented learners. Accreditation through NCATE is voluntary, and only those university programs choosing to seek accreditation must comply with the standards. Fewer than half the states require special certification for teachers of the gifted or formal university course work. Moreover, the majority of students with gifts and talents receive services from general education teachers. For these reasons, the PreK–12 schools have the greatest potential for improving services to gifted and talented learners by ensuring that the teachers who serve them meet the national standards. Responsibility for improving teaching and learning of gifted students—the end goal of professional standards for teachers of the gifted— resides ultimately with school personnel who hire teachers and ensure their competence by establishing selection criteria, providing professional development, and observing and assessing practice.

This chapter offers a brief history of the development of national standards for teachers of the gifted and identifies their importance to PreK–12 schools.

NATIONAL STANDARDS FOR PREPARATION OF TEACHERS OF THE GIFTED: HISTORY

Accreditation of teacher preparation programs provides recognition that programs meet national professional standards for teacher preparation through evidence of competent candidate performance. Setting standards for teacher preparation can be traced at least to 1922, when the International Council for the Education of Exceptional Children (now the Council for Exceptional Children, or CEC) began with 12 members and declared establishment of professional standards for special education as a fundamental aim (CEC, 2003). In 1927, the American Association of Teachers Colleges was organized to develop standards and accreditation procedures to ensure that graduates of accredited programs could teach (Kraft, 2001). In 1955, NCATE was founded as an affiliation of professional and public organizations and currently accredits over 600 colleges of education nationwide.

Robinson and Kolloff (2006) trace interest in competencies for teachers of the gifted to the early 1980s when the NAGC Professional Training Institutes engaged university faculty and practitioners in discussions of professional development issues and training guidelines. The new Professional Development Division established in 1987 continued this work by focusing on standards for graduate programs, given that most certification in gifted education occurs at the graduate level. A series of symposia resulted in the NAGC Standards for Graduate Programs in Gifted Education, approved as a position paper in 1995 and published in the *Gifted Child Quarterly* the next year (Parker, 1996). In 1998, the NAGC developed and adopted the PreK–12 Gifted Program Standards to assist school districts in designing and evaluating programs for gifted learners. These standards describe criteria for minimum and exemplary levels of quality related to program design, administration and management, student identification, socioemotional guidance and counseling, professional development, and program evaluation.

Meanwhile, the CEC and NCATE formed a partnership for approving training programs in 1976, and for many years, the CEC served as the sole special education affiliate. Through symposia and a research project, The Association for the Gifted, a division of the CEC, established standards in 1989 to encourage higher quality of the growing number of programs for gifted students. The standards addressed professional development of teachers, including course work for initial teacher preparation as well as program design, assessment for identification, and curriculum design for PreK–12 schools serving gifted learners.

In 1989, the CEC adopted a common core of standards with separate knowledge and skill items for the various areas of specialization (e.g., gifted, learning disabilities), which undergo periodic revision. The CEC's 10 common core standards and 137 knowledge and skill statements for preparation of teachers of the gifted have served as NCATE's national standards for university programs that prepare teachers of the gifted. Through a systematic process described below, these have been replaced by 10 revised standards and 70 knowledge and skill statements developed by the CEC-TAG and the NAGC for approval by NCATE in 2006.

In 2002, the NAGC became an affiliate of NCATE, and the NAGC and the CEC-TAG formed an interorganization work group to collaboratively revise the standards for preparation of teachers of the gifted. A series of symposia, work sessions, and review-and-comment activities between 2002 and 2006 resulted in an adaptation of the CEC's 10 core standards specifically for application to the field of gifted education and identification of 70 knowledge and skill statements that interpret and illustrate the core standards. The conceptual framework for the revised standards included Kraft's (2001) critical approach to standards analysis to identify standards that (a) move the field beyond the status quo, (b) reflect inclusive perspectives and values, (c) view standards as a means to the end of quality services to gifted learners and their families, and (d) develop autonomous, reflective practitioners. Additionally, the framework addressed TAG's (2001) *Diversity and Developing Gifts and Talents: A National Action Plan.*

The revised standards were approved in 2004 by the CEC-TAG and the NAGC for adoption by NCATE in 2006. Validation occurred through (a) compilation of research-, literature-, and practice-based publications supporting each knowledge and skill statement and (b) an electronic survey of stakeholders regarding perceptions of the importance of each knowledge and skill statement. University teacher preparation faculty and administrators, PreK–12 teachers and administrators, state directors of the gifted, researchers, and consultants in the United States and Canada from diverse ethnic backgrounds participated in this endeavor. The new standards represent a consensus of the two major professional organizations and a comprehensive range of constituents on what novice teachers of the gifted should know and be able to do.

IMPLICATIONS FOR PREK–12 SCHOOLS

The standards will be used to evaluate university programs seeking accreditation as meeting the national standards for preparation of teachers of the gifted. Higher education institutions that receive national accreditation for initial preparation of teachers of the gifted ensure that their graduates meet knowledge and skill standards developed and approved by the NAGC and TAG of the CEC. Yet not all universities seek national accreditation in gifted education. Despite the field's identification of evidence-based standards for preparation of teachers of the gifted, the fact remains that some states and universities have minimal or no requirements for formal teacher preparation in gifted education.

The most recent survey of 53 states and territories published by the NAGC and the Council of State Directors of Programs for the Gifted, *State of the States 2004–2005* report, indicated the following:

- Only one state, Washington, required course work in gifted education for regular classroom teachers (who serve the majority of gifted students).
- Twenty-three states required that teachers working in specialized programs for gifted and talented have taken graduate courses or received a teaching certificate in gifted education.
- State requirements for certification in gifted/talented education ranged from 6 credit hours (Arizona and South Carolina) to 24 (Colorado).
- Over 50% of state respondents identified professional development initiatives in gifted education (providing practical training for classroom teachers) as the most positive force affecting services for gifted students. (NAGC, 2006, p. 2)

Given differences among states and universities in requirements, how can school districts ensure that teachers provide the highest-quality instruction to gifted and talented learners? Clearly, while the national standards for preparation of teachers of the gifted were developed for university teacher preparation programs, the standards themselves were identified as what beginning teachers of the gifted need to know and be able to do in PreK–12 schools. The standards, then, can be used by districts as follows:

- To identify teachers for specialized positions working with gifted and talented students
- To identify general education teachers serving gifted and talented students
- To identify knowledge and skills for professional development of inservice teachers
- To identify expectations for local university-based teacher preparation programs
- To inform families about the specialized knowledge and skills needed by teachers of the gifted
- To advocate for state-level policies supporting certification of general and specialized teachers who work with gifted and talented learners

The purpose of this guidebook is to share with personnel responsible for professional development in PreK–12 schools the national standards for preparation of teachers of the gifted and suggest guidelines for their implementation with inservice teachers.

- Chapter 2 presents the 10 newly approved standards and 70 statements specifying the knowledge and skills involved in meeting the standards. It also summarizes the supporting literature base.
- Chapter 3 examines how the new standards for entry-level teachers of the gifted align with the national program standards currently used by districts to design and evaluate PreK–12 gifted programs.
- Chapter 4 overviews a general strategy for determining professional development needs based on the standards and training literature.

- Chapter 5 provides one approach to ensure that professional development objectives for teachers of the gifted and talented are integrated with gifted program standards and with other standards and policies important to the district (e.g., content standards).
- Chapter 6 offers a prescription for developing an effective professional development plan at the district level.
- Chapter 7 suggests professional development activities at the individual and school level.
- Chapter 8 identifies a number of effective strategies for assessing the outcomes of professional development activities.
- Chapter 9 focuses on the standards related to cultural diversity and professional development designed to address these standards.
- Chapter 10 examines challenges and opportunities for school districts as they implement the new standards.

2

Professional Standards for Teachers of Students With Gifts and Talents

Susan K. Johnsen

Standards are important to the field of gifted education. They define the essential knowledge and skills that teachers need to acquire to be effective in teaching gifted and talented students in the classroom. Knowledge is defined by "empirical research, disciplined inquiry, informed theory and the wisdom of practice" (National Council for Accreditation of Teacher Education [NCATE], 2006, pp. 57–59) and includes pedagogical, pedagogical content, and professional knowledge. Pedagogical content knowledge is the "interaction of the subject matter and effective teaching strategies to help students learn the subject matter," whereas "pedagogical knowledge is the general concepts, theories, and research about effective teaching, regardless of content areas" (p. 58). Professional knowledge includes the "understandings of schooling and education" from a multidisciplinary perspective and also "knowledge about learning, diversity, technology, professional ethics, legal and policy issues, pedagogy, and the roles and responsibilities of the profession of teaching" (p. 59). Skills are the "ability to use content, professional, and pedagogical knowledge effectively and readily in diverse teaching settings in a manner that ensures that all students are learning" (p. 56). Standards also help in gaining consensus among professionals who prepare future teachers and in achieving consistency across teacher preparation programs. They identify for others the legitimacy of gifted education not only in the area of teacher preparation but also as a separate field of study at the higher-education level based on a strong foundation of research (Darling-Hammond, Wise, & Klein, 1999; VanTassel-Baska, 2004; Yinger, 1999).

All of the 70 initial standards are organized into 10 Council for Exceptional Children (CEC) content standards: foundations, development and characteristics of learners, individual learning differences, instructional strategies, learning environments and social interactions, language and communication, instructional planning, assessment, professional and ethical practice, and collaboration. Professionals should use these standards when preparing professionals at the initial level.

NATIONAL ASSOCIATION FOR GIFTED CHILDREN AND COUNCIL FOR EXCEPTIONAL CHILDREN (TAG DIVISION) INITIAL STANDARDS: INDIVIDUALS WITH GIFTS AND TALENTS

Standard 1: Foundations

Educators of the gifted understand the field as an evolving and changing discipline based on philosophies, evidence-based principles and theories, relevant laws and policies, diverse and historical points of view, and human issues. These perspectives continue to influence the field of gifted education and the education and treatment of individuals with gifts and talents both in school and society. They recognize how foundational influences affect professional practice, including assessment, instructional planning, delivery, and program evaluation. They further understand how issues of human diversity impact families, cultures, and schools, and how these complex human issues can interact in the delivery of gifted and talented education services.

GT1K1: Historical foundations of gifted and talented education, including points of view and contributions of individuals from diverse backgrounds.

GT1K2: Key philosophies, theories, models, and research that supports gifted and talented education.

GT1K3: Local, state/provincial and federal laws and policies related to gifted and talented education.

GT1K4: Issues in conceptions, definitions, and identification of individuals with gifts and talents, including those of individuals from diverse backgrounds.

GT1K5: Impact of the dominant culture's role in shaping schools and the differences in values, languages, and customs between school and home.

GT1K6: Societal, cultural, and economic factors, including anti-intellectualism and equity versus excellence, enhancing or inhibiting the development of gifts and talents.

GT1K7: Key issues and trends, including diversity and inclusion, that connect general, special, and gifted and talented education.

Standard 2: Development and Characteristics of Learners

Educators of the gifted know and demonstrate respect for their students as unique human beings. They understand variations in characteristics and development between and among individuals with and without exceptional learning needs and capacities. Educators of the gifted can express how different characteristics interact with the domains of human development and use this knowledge to describe the varying abilities and behaviors of individuals with gifts and talents. Educators of the gifted also understand how families and communities contribute to the development of individuals with gifts and talents.

GT2K1: Cognitive and affective characteristics of individuals with gifts and talents, including those from diverse backgrounds, in intellectual, academic, creative, leadership, and artistic domains.

GT2K2: Characteristics and effects of culture and environment on the development of individuals with gifts and talents.

GT2K3: Role of families and communities in supporting the development of individuals with gifts and talents.

GT2K4: Advanced developmental milestones of individuals with gifts and talents from early childhood through adolescence.

GT2K5: Similarities and differences within the group of individuals with gifts and talents as compared to the general population.

Standard 3: Individual Learning Differences

Educators of the gifted understand the effects that gifts and talents can have on an individual's learning in school and throughout life. Moreover, educators of the gifted are active and resourceful in seeking to understand how language, culture, and family background interact with an individual's predispositions to impact academic and social behavior, attitudes, values, and interests. The understanding of these learning differences and their interactions provides the foundation upon which educators of the gifted plan instruction to provide meaningful and challenging learning.

GT3K1: Influences of diversity factors on individuals with gifts and talents.

GT3K2: Academic and affective characteristics and learning needs of individuals with gifts, talents, and disabilities.

GT3K3: Idiosyncratic learning patterns of individuals with gifts and talents, including those from diverse backgrounds.

GT3K4: Influences of different beliefs, traditions, and values across and within diverse groups on relationships among individuals with gifts and talents, their families, schools, and communities.

GT3S1: Integrate perspectives of diverse groups into planning instruction for individuals with gifts and talents.

Standard 4: Instructional Strategies

Educators of the gifted possess a repertoire of evidence-based curriculum and instructional strategies to differentiate for individuals with gifts and talents. They select, adapt, and use these strategies to promote challenging learning opportunities in general and special curricula and to modify learning environments to enhance self-awareness and self-efficacy for individuals with gifts and talents. They enhance the learning of critical and creative thinking, problem solving, and performance skills in specific domains. Moreover, educators of the gifted emphasize the development, practice, and transfer of advanced knowledge and skills across environments throughout the life span, leading to creative, productive careers in society for individuals with gifts and talents.

GT4K1: School and community resources, including content specialists, that support differentiation.

GT4K2: Curricular, instructional, and management strategies effective for individuals with exceptional learning needs.

GT4S1: Apply pedagogical content knowledge to instructing learners with gifts and talents.

GT4S2: Apply higher-level thinking and metacognitive models to content areas to meet the needs of individuals with gifts and talents.

GT4S3: Provide opportunities for individuals with gifts and talents to explore, develop, or research their areas of interest or talent.

GT4S4: Preassess the learning needs of individuals with gifts and talents in various domains and adjust instruction based on continual assessment.

GT4S5: Pace delivery of curriculum and instruction consistent with needs of individuals with gifts and talents.

GT4S6: Engage individuals with gifts and talents from all backgrounds in challenging, multicultural curricula.

GT4S7: Use information and/or assistive technologies to meet the needs of individuals with exceptional learning needs.

Standard 5: Learning Environments and Social Interactions

Educators of the gifted actively create learning environments for individuals with gifts and talents that foster cultural understanding, safety and emotional well-being, positive social interactions, and active engagement. In addition, educators of the gifted foster environments in which diversity is valued and individuals are taught to live harmoniously and productively in a culturally diverse world. Educators of the gifted shape environments to encourage independence, motivation, and self-advocacy of individuals with gifts and talents.

GT5K1: Ways in which groups are stereotyped and experience historical and current discrimination and implications for gifted and talented education.

GT5K2: Influence of social and emotional development on interpersonal relationships and learning of individuals with gifts and talents.

GT5S1: Design learning opportunities for individuals with gifts and talents that promote self-awareness, positive peer relationships, intercultural experiences, and leadership.

GT5S2: Create learning environments for individuals with gifts and talents that promote self-awareness, self-efficacy, leadership, and lifelong learning.

GT5S3: Create safe learning environments for individuals with gifts and talents that encourage active participation in individual and group activities to enhance independence, interdependence, and positive peer relationships.

GT5S4: Create learning environments and intercultural experiences that allow individuals with gifts and talents to appreciate their own and others' language and cultural heritage.

GT5S5: Develop social interaction and coping skills in individuals with gifts and talents to address personal and social issues, including discrimination and stereotyping.

Standard 6: Language and Communication

Educators of the gifted understand the role of language and communication in talent development and the ways in which exceptional conditions can hinder or facilitate such development. They use relevant strategies to teach oral and written communication skills to individuals with gifts and talents. Educators of the gifted are familiar with assistive technologies to support and enhance communication of individuals with exceptional needs. They match their communication methods to an individual's language proficiency and cultural and linguistic differences. Educators of the gifted use communication strategies and resources to facilitate understanding of subject matter for individuals with gifts and talents who are English language learners.

GT6K1: Forms and methods of communication essential to the education of individuals with gifts and talents, including those from diverse backgrounds.

GT6K2: Impact of diversity on communication.

GT6K3: Implications of culture, behavior, and language on the development of individuals with gifts and talents.

GT6S1: Access resources and develop strategies to enhance communication skills for individuals with gifts and talents, including those with advanced communication and/or English language learners.

GT6S2: Use advanced oral and written communication tools, including assistive technologies, to enhance the learning experiences of individuals with exceptional learning needs.

Standard 7: Instructional Planning

Curriculum and instructional planning is at the center of gifted and talented education. Educators of the gifted develop long-range plans anchored in both general and special curricula. They systematically translate shorter-range goals and objectives that take into consideration an individual's abilities and needs, the learning environment, and cultural and linguistic factors. Understanding of these factors, as well as the implications of being gifted and talented, guides the educator's selection, adaptation, and creation of materials, and use of differentiated instructional strategies. Learning plans are modified based on ongoing assessment of the individual's progress. Moreover, educators of the gifted facilitate these actions in a collaborative context that includes individuals with gifts and talents, families, professional colleagues, and personnel from other agencies as appropriate. Educators of the gifted are comfortable using technologies to support instructional planning and individualized instruction.

GT7K1: Theories and research models that form the basis of curriculum development and instructional practice for individuals with gifts and talents.

GT7K2: Features that distinguish differentiated curriculum from general curricula for individuals with exceptional learning needs.

GT7K3: Curriculum emphases for individuals with gifts and talents within cognitive, affective, aesthetic, social, and linguistic domains.

GT7S1: Align differentiated instructional plans with local, state/provincial, and national curricular standards.

GT7S2: Design differentiated learning plans for individuals with gifts and talents, including individuals from diverse backgrounds.

GT7S3: Develop scope and sequence plans for individuals with gifts and talents.

GT7S4: Select curriculum resources, strategies, and product options that respond to cultural, linguistic, and intellectual differences among individuals with gifts and talents.

GT7S5: Select and adapt a variety of differentiated curricula that incorporate advanced, conceptually challenging, in-depth, distinctive, and complex content.

GT7S6: Integrate academic and career guidance experiences into the learning plan for individuals with gifts and talents.

Standard 8: Assessment

Assessment is integral to the decision making and teaching of educators of the gifted as multiple types of assessment information are required for both identification and learning progress decisions. Educators of the gifted use the results of such assessments to adjust instruction and to enhance ongoing learning progress. Educators of the gifted understand the process of identification, legal policies, and ethical principles of measurement and assessment related to referral, eligibility, program planning, instruction, and placement for individuals with gifts and talents, including those from culturally and linguistically diverse backgrounds. They understand measurement theory and practices for addressing the interpretation of assessment results. In addition, educators of the gifted understand the appropriate use and limitations of various types of assessments. To ensure the use of nonbiased and equitable identification and learning progress models, educators of the gifted employ alternative assessments such as performance-based assessment, portfolios, and computer simulations.

GT8K1: Processes and procedures for the identification of individuals with gifts and talents.

GT8K2: Uses, limitations, and interpretation of multiple assessments in different domains for identifying individuals with exceptional learning needs, including those from diverse backgrounds.

GT8K3: Uses and limitations of assessments documenting academic growth of individuals with gifts and talents.

GT8S1: Use nonbiased and equitable approaches for identifying individuals with gifts and talents, including those from diverse backgrounds.

GT8S2: Use technically adequate qualitative and quantitative assessments for identifying and placing individuals with gifts and talents.

GT8S3: Develop differentiated curriculum-based assessments for use in instructional planning and delivery for individuals with gifts and talents.

GT8S4: Use alternative assessments and technologies to evaluate learning of individuals with gifts and talents.

Standard 9: Professional and Ethical Practice

Educators of the gifted are guided by the profession's ethical and professional practice standards. They practice in multiple roles and complex situations across wide age and developmental ranges. Their practice requires ongoing attention to professional and ethical considerations. They engage in professional activities that promote growth in individuals with gifts and talents and update themselves on evidence-based best practices. Educators of the gifted view themselves as lifelong learners and regularly reflect on and adjust their practice. They are aware of how attitudes, behaviors, and ways of communicating can influence their practice. Educators of the gifted understand that culture and language interact with gifts and talents and are sensitive to the many aspects of the diversity of individuals with gifts and talents and their families.

GT9K1: Personal and cultural frames of reference that affect one's teaching of individuals with gifts and talents, including biases about individuals from diverse backgrounds.

GT9K2: Organizations and publications relevant to the field of gifted and talented education.

GT9S1: Assess personal skills and limitations in teaching individuals with exceptional learning needs.

GT9S2: Maintain confidential communication about individuals with gifts and talents.

GT9S3: Encourage and model respect for the full range of diversity among individuals with gifts and talents.

GT9S4: Conduct activities in gifted and talented education in compliance with laws, policies, and standards of ethical practice.

GT9S5: Improve practice through continuous research-supported professional development in gifted education and related fields.

GT9S6: Participate in the activities of professional organizations related to gifted and talented education.

GT9S7: Reflect on personal practice to improve teaching and guide professional growth in gifted and talented education.

Standard 10: Collaboration

Educators of the gifted effectively collaborate with families, other educators, and related service providers. This collaboration enhances comprehensive articulated program options across educational levels and engagement of individuals with gifts and talents in meaningful learning activities and interactions. Moreover, educators of the gifted embrace their special role as advocate for individuals with gifts and talents. They promote and advocate for the learning and well-being of individuals with gifts and talents across settings and diverse learning experiences.

GT10K1: Culturally responsive behaviors that promote effective communication and collaboration with individuals with gifts and talents, their families, school personnel, and community members.

GT10S1: Respond to concerns of families of individuals with gifts and talents.

GT10S2: Collaborate with stakeholders outside the school setting who serve individuals with exceptional learning needs and their families.

GT10S3: Advocate for the benefit of individuals with gifts and talents and their families.

GT10S4: Collaborate with individuals with gifts and talents, their families, general and special educators, and other school staff to articulate a comprehensive preschool through secondary educational program.

GT10S5: Collaborate with families, community members, and professionals in assessment of individuals with gifts and talents.

GT10S6: Communicate and consult with school personnel about the characteristics and needs of individuals with gifts and talents, including individuals from diverse backgrounds.

KNOWLEDGE BASE FOR THE 10 CONTENT STANDARDS

Gifted education is a profession that has a strong research base and a formal body of knowledge that distinguishes it from other education professions and from the lay public. The CEC's Professional Standards and Practices Standing Committee (PSPSC) has organized this research into these three categories:

1. *Literature/theory based.* Knowledge or skills based on theories or philosophical reasoning. They include knowledge and skills derived from sources such as position papers, policy analyses, and descriptive reviews of the literature (PSPSC, 2003).

2. *Research based.* Knowledge or skills based on peer-reviewed studies that use appropriate research methodologies to address questions of cause and effect and that researchers have independently replicated and found to be effective (PSPSC, 2003).

3. *Practice based.* Knowledge and skills derived from a number of sources. Practices based on a small number of studies or nomination procedures, such as promising practices, are usually performance based. Practice-based knowledge or skills also include those derived primarily from model and lighthouse programs. Practice-based knowledge and skills include professional wisdom. These practices have been used so widely with practical evidence of effectiveness that there is an implicit professional assumption that the practice is effective. Practice-based knowledge and skills also include "emerging practice," practices that arise from teachers' classroom experiences validated through some degree of action research (PSPSC, 2003).

Using these definitions, the CEC-TAG/NAGC standards work group identified a minimum of at least three citations in each category for each standard. The following summaries of annotated references for each of the standards are meant to be representative, not exhaustive, and are not intended to endorse a particular theory, model, test, method, strategy, or material. A CD of the annotations is included with this guide.

Standard 1: Foundations Research Summary

Educators of the gifted understand that historical perspectives influence the field of gifted education, professional practice, and the treatment of individuals with gifts and talents.

- Conceptions of giftedness parallel the theoretical development of intelligence (Cattell, 1963; Galton, 1865; Gardner, 1983/1994; Guilford, 1967; Hollingworth, 1942; Sternberg, 1985; Terman, 1925).
- Creativity is viewed as distinctly different from convergent production (Guilford, 1967; Torrance, 1962).
- The field has moved from focusing only on individual characteristics of gifted students to interactions between genetic and environmental factors that influence performance (Csikszentmihalyi, 1988; Gardner, 1993; Hollingworth, 1942).
- Definitions have expanded from a focus on general intelligence to a variety of categories that include specific academic aptitude, leadership, creativity, and the arts (Marland, 1972; U.S. Department of Education, 1993).
- Researchers continue to examine other definitions that encompass school reform, the developmental nature of giftedness, domain-specific giftedness, and sociocultural context influences (Coleman, 2004; Feldman, 1980; Passow & Frasier, 1994; Renzulli, 2002).
- The majority of researchers view the concept of giftedness as more dynamic than static, with interventions required to develop above-average ability into exceptional performance (Bloom, 1985; Gagné, 1985; Sternberg, 2000; VanTassel-Baska, 1998).
- With only one federal law that addresses gifted education, states vary in conceptions, definitions, mandates, professional development requirements, and services (National Association for Gifted Children and the Council of State Directors of Programs for the Gifted, 2005; Stephens & Karnes, 2000).

- Given the different ways that giftedness is defined and manifested, new methods for identifying gifted and talented students from special populations are advocated (Borland & Wright, 1994; Johnsen, 2004; VanTassel-Baska, Johnson, & Avery, 2002).
- A variety of family, school, community, and personal factors influence students' achievement, particularly those from minority backgrounds (Castellano & Diaz, 2002; Diaz, 1998; Ford & Harris, 1997; Grantham & Ford, 1998; Harmon, 2002; Hébert, 1998; Ogbu, 1994).

Standard 2: Development and Characteristics of Learners

Educators of the gifted respect their students as individuals with unique characteristics.

- Theories distinguish gifted students from other nonidentified students (Cattell, 1971; Gardner, 1983/1994).
- Expert performance within a field is developed through catalysts and deliberate practice (Ericcson & Charness, 1994; Gagné, 2000).
- Gifted students are at least as well adjusted socially and emotionally as their nonidentified peers (Cross & Coleman, 1993; Neihart, 1999).
- Gifted individuals do experience life in a different way and report more perfectionism (Piechowski, 1992; Roberts & Lovett, 1994; Schuler, 2000).
- While gifted students generally are well adjusted, some experience asynchronous development that may contribute to social problems and may suggest a need to address the affective needs of gifted students (Hébert, 1991; Silverman, 1997).
- Culture plays a role in the development of talent and is mediated by the individual's performance and cognitive style (Shade, 1997).
- The family assumes a role in the development of talent, with teachers and adults in the community serving as a primary influence for children who are from economically disadvantaged backgrounds (Moon, Jurich, & Feldhusen, 1998; VanTassel-Baska, Olszewski-Kubilius, & Kulieke, 1994).
- Because of advanced functioning, teachers need to provide intellectual challenge in their classrooms and foster an environment that values different cultures, provides access to mentors, and gives students a voice in their learning process (Ablard & Tissot, 1998; Grantham & Ford, 1998; Gross, 2002; Hughes, 1999; Hébert & Neumeister, 2000; Kanevsky & Keighley, 2003; Lupkowski-Shoplik & Assouline, 1994; Lynch, 1992; McLaughlin & Saccuzzo, 1997; Moon & Callahan, 2001; Robinson & Clinkenbeard, 1998; Winner & Martino, 2000).

Standard 3: Individual Learning Differences

Educators of gifted students understand that language, culture, and family background interact with individual dispositions to impact academic and social behavior, attitudes, values, and interests, and they tailor gifted instruction to provide meaningful learning experiences.

- Gifted students' learning and achievement can be affected by diversity issues, including race, culture and language, sex, sexual orientation, poverty, learning style, personality, and/or having a disability (Benbow, Lubinski, Shea, & Eftekhari-Sanjani, 2000; Garrison, 1993; Good, Aronson, & Inzlicht, 2003; Kerr & Kurpius, 2004; Ogbu, 1995; Peterson & Rischar, 2000; Piirto, 1998; Stormont, Stebbins, & Holliday, 2001).

- Family background influences a gifted student's abilities and achievement (Albert, 1996; Hunsaker, 1995; Renzulli & Park, 2002; Solow, 1995).
- Since diversity influences student behavior, educators need to consider alternative assessment procedures and instructional strategies (Artiles & Zamora-Duran, 1997; Barkan & Bernal, 1991; Belcher & Fletcher-Carter, 1999; Hébert, 2002; Kirschenbaum, 2004; Kitano & Espinosa, 1995; Matthews & Matthews, 2004; VanTassel-Baska, Johnson, & Avery, 2002).
- Educators need to be sensitive to the gifted student's affective needs because of mismatches between educational and home environments, self-image, and the level of a gifted student's learning ability (Delisle & Galbraith, 2002; Grantham & Ford, 2003; Greene, 2003; Mendaglio, 1995).
- Underachievement is influenced by the level of challenge in the classroom and social, cultural, and psychological factors in the life of the diverse gifted student (Baum, Renzulli, & Hébert, 1995; Emerick, 1992; Ford & Thomas, 1997; Johnson, 1994).

Standard 4: Instructional Strategies

Educators of the gifted select, adapt, and use evidence-based curriculum and instructional strategies to differentiate learning environments that will challenge gifted learners.

- Three factors need to be present for students to develop their talents: (a) above-average ability and motivation; (b) school, community, and/or family support; and (c) acceptance by peers in the domain of talent (Bloom, 1985; Csikszentmihalyi, 1996; Gagné, 2003; Renzulli, 1994; Siegle & McCoach, 2005).
- Teachers need to use metacognitive and higher-level thinking strategies in the content areas, provide activities that address the gifted students' areas of interest, and foster research skills (Anderson & Krathwohl, 2001; Center for Gifted Education, 2000; Elder & Paul, 2003; Hébert, 1993; Johnsen & Goree, 2005; Moon, Feldhusen, & Dillon, 1994; VanTassel-Baska, Avery, Little, & Hughes, 2000).
- Curriculum strategies for gifted students include acceleration, enrichment, grouping, problem-based learning, curriculum compacting, specific curriculum models, and extracurricular activities (Colangelo, Assouline, & Gross, 2004; Gallagher & Stepien, 1996; Gentry, 1999; Kulik & Kulik, 1992; Milgram, Hong, Shavit, & Peled, 1997; Reis, Burns, & Renzulli, 1992; Renzulli & Reis, 2003, 2004; Rogers, 1991; Southern & Jones, 1991; Tomlinson & Cunningham-Eidson, 2003; Tomlinson et al., 2001; VanTassel-Baska & Little, 2003).
- Educators may use preassessment to guide adjustments to instruction to sustain the individual student's progress (Reis, et al., 1992; Winebrenner, 2003).
- Technology can be used in independent studies to access mentors and resources, and to enroll in advanced classes (Cross, 2004; Ravaglia, Suppes, Stillinger, & Alper, 1995; Siegle, 2004).
- When individuals from diverse backgrounds are provided challenging curricula, they are more likely to qualify for gifted programming and reduce underachievement (Ford, 1996; Ford & Harris, 1997; Mills, Stork, & Krug, 1992).

Standard 5: Learning Environments and Social Interactions

Educators of the gifted strive to provide learning environments that value diversity, emotional well-being, positive social interactions, and engagement both in the present and in the future.

- Stereotypes can hinder test performance, healthy attitudes toward school subjects, and successful progress (Hyde, Fennema, Ryan, & Frost, 1990; Kitano & Perkins, 1996; Perry, Steele, & Hilliard, 2003; Steele, 1997).
- The classroom needs to be a place where gifted students can learn about and respect different social and cultural norms and language diversity (Gay, 2002).
- Factors that contribute to high-ability students becoming at risk are heightened emotional sensitivity, lack of nurturing, abuse, low self-esteem, perfectionism, and unrealistic parental expectations (Dixon, Lapsley, & Hanchon, 2004; Moon, 2004).
- Since emotional maturity is needed to actualize individual abilities, counseling programs need to focus on prevention instead of remediation (Landau & Weissler, 1998).
- Educators need to be receptive to gifted students' affective needs and sensitive to the socioemotional and coping needs of special groups (Albert & Runco, 1989; Cline & Schwartz, 1999; Cross, Stewart, & Coleman, 2003; Ford & Harris, 2000; Gross, 2003; Kerr & Cohn, 2001; Lovecky, 1995; Perry et al., 2003; Peterson, 2003).
- Video therapy, bibliotherapy, and affective curricula are strategies that can be used in the classroom (Hébert, 1991; Milne & Reis, 2000; Peterson, 2003).
- Working in groups with other gifted students and mentors can yield academic benefits and enhance self-confidence and communication skills (Brody, 1999; Davalos & Haensly, 1997; Grybe, 1997; Pleiss & Feldhusen, 1995; Torrance, 1984).
- Other learning situations that support self-efficacy, creativity, and lifelong learning include early college entrance programs, talent searches, competitions, problem-based learning, independent play, independent study, and the International Baccalaureate Program (Betts, 2004; Boothe, Sethna, Stanley, & Colgate, 1999; Christophersen & Mortweet, 2003; Gallagher, 1997; Johnsen & Goree, 2005; Olszewski-Kubilius, 1998; Poelzer & Feldhusen, 1997; Riley & Karnes, 1998; Rotigel & Lupkowski-Shoplik, 1999).

Standard 6: Language and Communication

Educators of the gifted understand the role of language and communication in talent development and the role that it plays for English language learners in the school setting.

- Educators can provide verbal development in gifted students by differentiating the curriculum, training in private speech, analogical reasoning, leadership, public speaking, writing, self-advocacy, and empathy (Castillo, 1998; Choi, 1998; Daugherty, White, & Manning, 1994; Feldhusen & Kennedy, 1988; Frey, 1998, 2000; Ingram, 2003; Karnes, Meriweather, & D'Ilio, 1987; VanTassel-Baska, Johnson, Hughes, & Boyce, 1996; VanTassel-Baska, Zuo, Avery, & Little, 2002).
- Studying other languages can contribute to higher English reading scores, higher verbal and grammar scores, and understanding of figurative speech

during the process of translation (Thompson & Thompson, 1996; van Stekelenburg, 1984; VanTassel-Baska, 1982, 2003d).

- Socioeconomic and linguistic differences can affect verbal performance and put English language learners at a disadvantage of being identified for gifted programs (Fernández, Gay, Lucky, & Gavilan, 1998; Tyler-Wood & Carri, 1993).
- Holistic identification procedures using local norms and bilingual programs may increase the number of English language learners in gifted programs (Kitano & Espinosa, 1995; Kolesinski & Leroux, 1992; Reyes, Fletcher & Paez, 1996).
- Educators should use research-based strategies for instructing English language learners and view multilingualism as a strength (Kitano & Pedersen, 2002b; Valdes, 2002).
- Strategies that can foster open communication between teachers and parents of English language learners are (a) encouraging parent participation, (b) providing parent workshops, and (c) professional development of preservice teachers (Rash, 1998; Riley, 1999; Stephens, 1999).

Standard 7: Instructional Planning

Curriculum and instructional planning is a central part of gifted education.

- Different models that form the basis of curriculum development and instructional practice include acceleration, autonomous learning, the Integrated Curriculum Model, the Parallel Curriculum Model, layered curriculum, the Purdue Three-Stage Model, the Schoolwide Enrichment Model, the Triarchic Model, and Talents Unlimited (Betts & Neihart, 1986; Kaplan, 2005; Moon et al., 1994; Renzulli & Reis, 2003; Schlichter & Palmer, 1993; Southern & Jones, 1991; Sternberg, Torff, & Grigorenko, 1998; Tomlinson et al., 2001; VanTassel-Baska & Stambaugh, 2006a).
- Models emphasize the need for considering students' interests, environmental and natural catalysts, curriculum differentiation, and the development of higher-level thinking skills (Elder & Paul, 2003; Gagné, 1995; Renzulli & Reis, 2003; Tomlinson & Cunningham-Eidson, 2003).
- Gifted students' cultural, linguistic, and intellectual differences should be considered when planning instruction and differentiating curriculum (Boothe & Stanley, 2004).
- Multicultural literature can be used to build respect across students' cultures and improve standardized test scores (Norton & Norton, 2002; Uresti, Goertz, & Bernal, 2002).
- Characteristics of differentiated curriculum include acceleration, curriculum compacting, different goals and outcomes, grouping, multiple menus, modular and supplementary materials, problem-based learning, independent study, and tiered lessons (Gallagher & Stepien, 1996; Johnson, Boyce, & VanTassel-Baska, 1995; Johnsen & Goree, 2005; Reis et al., 1992; Renzulli, Leppien, & Hays, 2000; Rogers, 2002; Southern & Jones, 1991; Tomlinson, 2002; VanTassel-Baska & Stambaugh, 2006a).
- Career guidance should be integrated into learning plans for gifted students, particularly those from diverse backgrounds (Cline & Schwartz, 1999; Kerr & Sodano, 2003).

- Differentiated curricula results in increased student engagement, enhanced reasoning skills, and improved habits of mind (VanTassel-Baska et al., 2000).
- Specific curricula have been designed for gifted students and include affective education, leadership, domain-specific studies, and the arts (Clark & Zimmerman, 1997; Nugent, 2005; Parker & Begnaud, 2003; VanTassel-Baska, 2003b).

Standard 8: Assessment

For gifted educators, assessments are vital for decision making when working with gifted students in terms of identification, monitoring academic process, and adjusting instruction.

- Researchers have suggested using multiple measures and alternative assessments in the identification process since different groups of children have different areas of gifts and talents (Frasier, 1991; Reid, Romanoff, Algozzine, & Udall, 2000).
- Specific assessments have been designed that measure creativity, music and dance, visual arts, leadership, domain-specific areas, and general intelligence (Clark, 2004; Hunsaker & Callahan, 1995; Karnes et al., 1987; Oreck, Owen, & Baum, 2003; Torrance, 1984).
- Schools' identification procedures should match program services and be evaluated to determine their effectiveness in identifying gifted students (Feldhusen, Asher, & Hoover, 2004; Johnsen, 2004; VanTassel-Baska, 2004).
- Assessments suggested for identification of gifted students, particularly those from culturally and linguistically diverse backgrounds, include dynamic assessment, peer nomination, nonverbal tests, alternative screenings, performance assessment, problem-based tasks, observations, and other qualitative methods (Borland & Wright, 1994; Kirschenbaum, 2004; Maker, 1994; Rogers, 1998; VanTassel-Baska et al., 2002).
- When identifying minority students, teachers need to be trained to assess language proficiency, examine tests for bias, and look for factors other than "school house giftedness" (Baldwin, 2002; Ford, 2004b; Zamora-Duran & Reyes, 1997).
- Assessments used to document academic growth include authentic tasks, portfolios, and rubrics and performance-based assessments (Siegle, 2002; Treffinger, 1994; VanTassel-Baska, 2002).
- The results of progress assessments can be used to adjust instruction, including placement in appropriate group learning settings and academic acceleration (Feldhusen, 1996; Kulik, 1992).

Standard 9: Professional and Ethical Practice Research Summary

Educators of the gifted are guided by the ethical and professional practice standards of the profession.

- Teachers' personal and cultural frames of reference may influence their identification of gifted and talented students (Frasier et al., 1995; Masten & Plata, 2000; Peterson & Margolin, 1997).

- Since teacher's biases and a lack of understanding about different cultures may also affect their teaching of gifted minority students, they need training in multicultural characteristics (Ford & Trotman, 2001).
- Teachers with gifted education training demonstrated greater teaching skills and developed more positive classroom climates (Hansen & Feldhusen, 1994).
- Gifted education teachers need to discriminate between caring and confidential conversations in a school setting, exhibit qualified employee behaviors in the workplace, and know the code of ethics of their professions (Council for Exceptional Children, 2003; Keller, 1999; Morehead, 1998).
- Teachers of the gifted should be familiar with state identification policies and the legal framework in which gifted services are to be provided (Coleman & Gallagher, 1995; Karnes & Marquardt, 1997a).
- Educators of the gifted should diligently improve their practice through research-supported professional development and reflection (Callahan, Cooper, & Glascock, 2003; Gubbins et al., 2002).
- The Association for the Gifted of the Council for Exceptional Children and the National Association for Gifted Children support professional development and advocate appropriate governmental policies for gifted students.
- Publications in the field of gifted education include *Gifted Child Quarterly*, *Gifted Child Today*, *Gifted Education International*, *Journal of Advanced Academics*, *Journal for the Education of the Gifted*, *Journal of Secondary Gifted Education* (discontinued in 2006), *Parenting for High Potential*, *Teaching for High Potential*, *Understanding Our Gifted*, and *Roeper Review*.

Standard 10: Collaboration

Collaboration among educators of the gifted, families, other educators, and related service providers facilitates successful transitions for gifted students among levels of their schooling process.

- Teachers can work with parents and one another in developing and implementing services for gifted children and maintaining current knowledge about best practices in the field (Kingore, 1995; Landrum, 2003; Parker, 1996; Strip & Hirsch, 2001).
- While parents can detect early signs of giftedness in their young children, they may be reluctant to seek educational options from the school (Hertzog & Bennett, 2004; Louis & Lewis, 1992; Olszewski-Kubilius & Lee, 2004; Pletan, Robinson, Berninger, & Abbot, 1995).
- Parent education programs are one way to disseminate information about gifted children and need to be carefully planned to be effective (Pearl, 1997; Stephens, 1999).
- Teachers need to collaborate with the community in providing other types of learning opportunities, such as through museums and universities and with mentors who can be a critical factor in motivating students to take advanced courses, identifying careers, and developing professional networks (Melber, 2003; Miserandino, Subotnik, & Ou, 1995; Myers, 1993/1994; Reilly & Welch, 1994/1995; Terry, 2003).

- Collaboration with schools and companies overseas can allow for studying abroad, which may broaden gifted students' perspectives on families, schools, and communities (Limburg-Weber, 1999/2000).
- Teachers need to collaborate with special education teachers and parents in providing services to gifted students with disabilities and in removing social and institutional obstacles for minority students (Kitano, 1997; VanTassel-Baska, 1992).
- As long as gifted education is not protected by federal and state mandates, vigorous advocacy and organized collaboration among gifted educators, administration, and parents is essential for change to occur (Hertzog, 2003; Irvine, 1991; Karnes & Marquardt, 1997b; Ridges, 2000; Ross, 1991; Shaklee, Padak, Barton, & Johnson, 1991).

3

Aligning Teacher Preparation Standards and NAGC PreK–12 Gifted Program Standards

Joyce VanTassel-Baska

As noted in Chapter 1, the National Association for Gifted Children (NAGC) developed PreK–12 Gifted Program Standards in 1998 to assist school districts in evaluating the quality of their programming for gifted students. The program standards define minimum and exemplary standards in seven areas: program design, program administration and management, student identification, curriculum and instruction, socioemotional guidance and counseling, professional development, and program evaluation. A brochure containing the detailed framework can be downloaded from the NAGC Web site, www.nagc.org. The national standards for teachers of the gifted (Chapter 2) serve an important function in preparing educators to work effectively with gifted learners. These two sets of standards share common ground with respect to several areas of emphasis. Both sets of standards reflect an attempt to reach consensus about the field of gifted education and how it should function in order to grow and develop. Both sets of standards reflect the judgment of a collaborative of professionals working together to create a template for practice. Finally, both sets of standards address a comprehensive way of developing programs, one in teacher education at universities and the other in PreK–12 schools, with underlying support guides to aid professionals in their work.

Yet the standard sets also diverge in particular ways: (a) The new teacher education standards were developed across organizations, whereas the NAGC standards were particular to that organization. (b) The teacher education standards have a documented research base for each indicator, whereas there is no corollary research base for the program standards to date. (c) The teacher education standards are one set that represents a level of proficiency to be attained, whereas the PreK–12 program standards contain both a minimum and exemplary level of attainment with different indicators for each level. (d) The program standards were developed in 1998, whereas the newer teacher education standards were finally approved by NCATE in 2006. This chapter examines how the new standards for teachers of the gifted align with the national program standards and makes recommendations for change.

Given the differences between the two standard sets in purpose and development, the alignment process for seeing the relationships between the sets must be approached with caution. It is clear from this work that the program standards will need to be upgraded and more systematically aligned with the research-based teacher education standards to ensure coherence at both the university and school district level in respect to personnel and program development.

The process used for alignment may be seen in Table 3.1 where the program standards are listed on the horizontal axis and the teacher education standards on the vertical axis. A brief explanation of each intersection follows, along with an analysis of where alignment is lacking.

The NAGC program standards align best with the foundations standard and its underlying indicators for teacher education. The strongest match is in the area of knowledge about gifted education policies and the acknowledgment of the need for a sound research base for program design work. The emphasis in program design on flexible grouping and differentiation align better with the instructional planning standard for teacher education and the development and characteristics of learners, which serves as an important basis for program design. Funding issues are not addressed in the teacher education standards.

The administration and management standards in their emphasis on qualified personnel can be seen as a more general version of the entire teacher education standards that define what qualified personnel should be. Beyond that indicator, however, the standards are seen to some extent in the teacher education collaboration standard and the professional and ethical practice standard. The integration with general education could be linked back to foundations and/or to the development and characteristics of learners standards in its underlying emphasis on similarities and differences to typical learners.

The identification standards map quite well with the assessment standard in the teacher education set. However, they are not cast in language broad enough to include assessment of learning. Both sets of standards stress equitable processes and procedures, research-based approaches, and the use of multiple methods.

The NAGC curriculum and instruction program standards are crafted at a more general level than comparable indicators in the teacher education standards. While an emphasis on differentiation forms of acceleration and the need for a continuum of options is stressed, no specifics are offered in respect to what these elements might be in operationalized form. The instructional strategy and the instructional planning standards together represent a more comprehensive look at what is needed in this area. The intent of both sets of standards, however, appears to be similar. The teacher education standards are just more explicit in respect to identifying key strategies and procedures to be effected.

The socioemotional standard emphasizes the need for differentiated guidance and career preparation as well as addressing problems of underachievement and at-risk youth through an affective curriculum. These issues are addressed in the teacher education standards in three different places. The individual learning differences standard addresses differential characteristics in the affective realm and emphasizes the need to address student diversity. The learning environments and social interaction standard addresses specific components of a differentiated guidance program. The instructional planning standard addresses the need for academic and career counseling.

The NAGC professional development standards stress the need for qualified personnel who have time to plan for the needs of gifted learners and who have the opportunity to improve their practice through a comprehensive plan for professional development. The corollary standard in the teacher education set is professional and ethical practice where there is an emphasis on self-assessment and reflective practice as a basis for building one's own professional development plan in conjunction with membership in relevant professional organizations.

The standards on program evaluation in the NAGC program set is a brief listing of general principles for conducting evaluations. There is no analogue for the indicators in the new teacher education standards. Program evaluation was seen to be a more advanced set of skills reserved for work in advanced programs in gifted education rather than the initial licensure program, although the assessment standard addresses ways to judge the learning of gifted students, which is the heart of a strong program evaluation.

Based on this analysis, there is a clear need to bring the NAGC program standards into closer alignment with the teacher education standards in key areas. Perhaps the standards most out of alignment are the following: program design, professional development, and program evaluation. Moreover, key themes pervade the new teacher education standards that are missing from the program standards. These themes are technology and diversity. Little mention is made of these areas in the program standards even though they are central to a vision of gifted program development in schools. In the areas of curriculum and instruction and socioemotional development, the new standards provide greater specificity for the indicators outlined in the NAGC standards but are not fundamentally unaligned. Identification standards are most closely aligned, and the administration and management are reasonably so, with a strong emphasis on qualified personnel. The standards task force could easily effect the alignment needed in the NAGC program standards as a next step in the process.

The program standards for gifted education must be aligned with the overarching teacher education standards to ensure the coherent translation of theory and research to the world of practice. This chapter points the way to how that process can occur and what yet remains to be done. Teacher preparation and exemplary programs and services are hand-in-glove operations that require integration of understandings and skills on the part of both teachers of the gifted and program coordinators.

Table 3.1 Aligning Teacher Preparation and PreK–12 Gifted Program Standards

NAGC Standards–Gifted Program Standards, PreK–12	Program Design	Admin and Management	Student Identification	Curriculum and Instruction	Socioemotional Guidance	Professional Development	Program Evaluation
NAGC-CEC Teacher Knowledge and Skills Standards for Gifted and Talented Education	1. Continuum of services 2. Adequate funding 3. Comprehensive base 4. Integration into general education 5. Student groupings & differentiated instruction 6. Specific policies for adaptations	1. Qualified personnel 2. Integration with general education 3. Collaboration with other agencies & parents of students 4. Resources & materials to support program	1. Comprehensive nominations 2. Measurement of diverse abilities 3. Individual assessment profiles 4. Based on current research 5. Specific written procedures	1. Differentiated for K–12 2. C. & I. adaptation to meet needs 3. Flexible instructional pacing 4. Provisions for educational "skipping" 5. Continuum of differentiated options	1. Differentiated guidance to meet needs 2. Career guidance services 3. Guidance for those at risk 4. Provisions for affective curriculum 5. Inclusion for underachieving	1. Comprehensive staff development 2. Ensure qualified instructor training 3. Support relating to gifted program 4. Time/support for preparation & development	1. Must be purposeful 2. Must be economic 3. Ensure competent & ethical standards 4. Availability of evaluation through written report
Standard 1: Foundations	K1 Historical foundations K2 Key support in theory & research K3 Related policies K4 ID of gifts and talents K5 Impact of dominant culture K6 Societal factors involved K7 Key issues and trends						

NAGC Standards–Gifted Program Standards, PreK–12	Program Design	Admin and Management	Student Identification	Curriculum and Instruction	Socioemotional Guidance	Professional Development	Program Evaluation
Standard 2: Development & Characteristics of Learners	K1 Cognitive & affective characteristics of individuals K2 Characteristics of environment K3 Roles of families and communities K4 Advanced developmental milestones	K5 Similarities & differences between gifted and general groups					
Standard 3: Individual Learning Differences					K1 Influences of diversity factors K2 Academic & affective characteristics K3 Idiosyncratic learning patterns K4 Influences of different beliefs, traditions, and values S1 Integration of perspectives		
Standard 4: Instructional Strategies				K1 School & community resources K2 Effective learning strategies S1 Apply pedagogical content to instruction			

(Continued)

Table 3.1 (Continued)

NAGC Standards–Gifted Program Standards, PreK–12	Program Design	Admin and Management	Student Identification	Curriculum and Instruction	Socioemotional Guidance	Professional Development	Program Evaluation
Standard 4 (cont.)				S2 Apply metacognition to content areas S3 Provide opportunities for exploration S4 Preassess learning needs S5 Pace delivery of curriculum S6 Provide engaging, multicultural curricula S7 Use technologies to meet learning needs			
Standard 5: Learning Environments & Social Interactions					K1 Implications of stereotypes, discrimination K2 Influence of social-emotional development S1 promote self awareness, & positive relationships S2 Promote self-efficacy and lifelong learning S3 Create safe learning environments		

NAGC Standards– Gifted Program Standards, PreK–12	Program Design	Admin and Management	Student Identification	Curriculum and Instruction	Socioemotional Guidance	Professional Development	Program Evaluation
					S4 Create intercultural experiences S5 Develop coping skills & social interaction		
Standard 6: Language & Communication				K1 Essential forms & methods of communication K2 Impact of diversity on communication K3 Implications of culture, behavior, & language S1 Access resources to enhance communication S2 Use advance oral and written communication tools			
Standard 7: Instructional Planning				K1 Theory & research behind basis of curriculum K2 Features of differentiated curriculum K3 Emphasis in cognitive, affective, aesthetic, social, and linguistic domains	S6 Integrate academic & career experiences into learning plans		

(Continued)

Table 3.1 (Continued)

NAGC Standards–Gifted Program Standards, PreK–12	Program Design	Admin and Management	Student Identification	Curriculum and Instruction	Socioemotional Guidance	Professional Development	Program Evaluation
Standard 7 (cont.)				S1 Align instructional plans with local regulations S2 Design plans that allow for multiple cultures S3 Develop scope & sequence plans S4 Select resources that address multiple cultures S5 Select curricula that is challenging, distinct, & complex			
Standard 8: Assessment			K1 Identification procedures and models K2 Uses, limitations, & interpretation of assessments K3 Uses & limitations with academic growth S1 Use of nonbiased, equitable approaches S2 Use of adequate assessment for identification				

NAGC Standards–Gifted Program Standards, PreK–12	Program Design	Admin and Management	Student Identification	Curriculum and Instruction	Socioemotional Guidance	Professional Development	Program Evaluation
			S3 Develop differentiated curriculum-based assessments S4 Use alternative assessments and technologies				
Standard 9: Professional & Ethical Practice						K1 Awareness of one's own personal & cultural frames of reference K2 Use of relevant publications and organizations S1 Assess personal skills and limitations S2 Maintain confidentiality S3 Encourage and model respect S4 Comply with laws and policies regarding ethical practice S5 Improve through continuous professional development S6 Participate in professional activities S7 Reflect on personal practices	

(Continued)

Table 3.1 (Continued)

NAGC Standards–Gifted Program Standards, PreK–12	Program Design	Admin and Management	Student Identification	Curriculum and Instruction	Socioemotional Guidance	Professional Development	Program Evaluation
Standard 10: Collaboration		K1 Culturally responsive behaviors to promote communication S1 Respond to families' concerns S2 Collaborate with stakeholders outside the school S3 Advocate for individuals S4 Collaborate with individuals and their families S5 Collaborate with families and communities in assessment S6 Consult with school personnel about needs and characteristics of individuals					

4

Sensing and Assessing Teacher Needs

Margie Kitano

The literature summarized in Chapter 2 provides a convincing argument in support of standards for the initial preparation of teachers of the gifted. Few practicing teachers actually adapt instruction for gifted learners (Robinson & Kolloff, 2006). Accommodating the needs of gifted learners requires more than a single introductory course (Bain, Bourgeois, & Pappas, 2003), and formal preparation promotes effective instruction as well as a positive classroom environment for high-ability students (Hansen & Feldhusen, 1994). Because many gifted students attend general education classes, all teachers require knowledge and skills in gifted education (Callahan, Cooper, & Glascock, 2003). Moreover, well-designed professional development can correct teacher misconceptions and enable teachers to implement newly acquired curriculum and instructional strategies (Gubbins et al., 2002; VanTassel-Baska & Stambaugh, 2006b).

How might a school district incorporate the standards in professional development activities? The optimistic premise is that beginning teachers of the gifted should demonstrate all the knowledge and skill items associated with the 10 standards. However, entry-level teachers' mastery of the standards varies based on preservice preparation in gifted education as well as state and district requirements for teachers of the gifted. Teacher needs also differ based on their setting (general classroom, enrichment cluster, pullout, self-contained), grade level, content area, and students served (highly gifted, gifted English language learners, gifted students with disabilities).

Districts desiring to orient large numbers of teachers who are new to the field might design content based on the identified districtwide needs. In contrast, districts that require university certification in gifted education for beginning teachers of the gifted may encourage teachers to pursue development more independently through individual professional plans (e.g., Karnes & Shaunessy, 2004). Districts may combine these two approaches to ensure a common core of knowledge and skills as well as opportunities for teachers to address issues specific to their sites and professional interests. By providing a range of options and choices, staff developers model accommodation for individual learning needs as opposed to a one-size-fits-all strategy. This chapter summarizes recommendations from the literature for standards-based identification of professional development needs for both districts and individual teachers.

DISTRICTWIDE PROFESSIONAL DEVELOPMENT PLANNING

Districts can identify and prioritize teachers' professional development needs through two complementary processes: needs sensing and needs assessment (Dettmer, Landrum, & Miller, 2006).

Needs Sensing

Dettmer et al. (2006) define needs sensing as a precursor to needs assessment and as a way of evaluating readiness for district-identified themes. Strategies include informal interviews and dialogues with individuals or small groups, classroom observations, visits to other programs, analyses of requests for materials and other resources, and anecdotal comments from a variety of stakeholders, including families. Rossett and Sheldon (2001) describe this first phase as performance analysis, a "scoping, a reconnaissance effort used to determine what is needed" (p. 31).

Needs Assessment

Needs assessment involves more formal data collection through structured interviews, surveys, checklists, questionnaires, and focus groups. Questions should be structured to provide information useful for designing and developing the program and materials. Dettmer et al. (2006) note that teachers' participation in formal needs assessment and decision making based on results enhances their ownership of professional development activities.

Steps

In practice, needs sensing and needs assessment overlap. Leaders of gifted and talented programs can provide direction for professional development through a series of iterative steps adapted from the training literature (Rossett & Sheldon, 2001).

1. *Sensing the larger context.* District-level professional development staff who have access to student achievement and other data and who interact with teachers and administrators across school sites have the advantage of a "big picture" perspective. They may be the first to perceive emerging trends with implications for professional development. For example, inspection of districtwide student data may

reveal achievement gaps among specific groups of gifted students. Visits with principals and teachers may suggest increased identification of gifted students with specific disabilities. It is important that the reviewed data on student outcomes match the program goals, which may identify an achievement expectation (e.g., 99th percentile on a standardized achievement test in the talent area; increased critical thinking or self-efficacy). Data gleaned from needs sensing can be categorized by standard: Do the needs seem related to Foundations in gifted education (Standard 1), Development and Characteristics of Gifted Learners (Standard 2), Individual Learning Differences (Standard 3), Instructional Strategies (Standard 4), Learning Environments and Social Interactions (Standard 5), Language and Communication (Standard 6), Instructional Planning (Standard 7), Assessment (Standard 8), Professional and Ethical Practice (Standard 9), and/or Collaboration (Standard 10)?

2. *Targeting directions.* Rossett and Sheldon (2001) describe this step as determining the desired future state. For gifted and talented programs, the desired situation might be that (a) all teachers, programs, and students meet their respective national, state, and district standards and (b) gifted students across economic, gender, ethnic, and ability/disability groups achieve at the highest levels in their areas of talent.

3. *Identifying "drivers."* Rossett and Sheldon (2001) encourage leaders to determine the drivers, or what it will take to realize the desired future state. Why isn't the district there now? What will it take? What are the potential obstacles? Needs sensing, focus groups, and formal needs assessment should include questions designed to identify drivers and impediments.

4. *Determining current status.* At this stage, program leaders gauge the district's current situation with respect to the targeted direction and factors influencing that direction. Two types of assessment are useful, and for different purposes: (a) independently observed indicators of current status and (b) more subjective teacher perceptions of needs.

Independent observations. Consider, for example, a district whose direction concerns improved achievement outcomes supported by effective curriculum and instruction with appropriately high levels of expectation and challenge. Research demonstrates considerable differences between *actual* and *perceived* needs (VanTassel-Baska, 2003c), with actual needs determined through systematic in-classroom observations and student outcomes. Assessments of teachers' *perceptions* of needs may measure what teachers believe they know rather than what they actually do in the classroom. Robinson and Kolloff's (2006) review of literature on classroom practices indicated that teachers may not implement strategies they recognize as appropriate for gifted students and may believe they are implementing them more than their students perceive them to be. An observational study of teachers of the gifted demonstrated need for emphasis on use of strategies for individualization, critical thinking, problem solving, and metacognition (VanTassel-Baska, 2003c).

Observations of teachers and students in the classroom, then, help identify actual professional development needs. Several validated observation instruments have been published (Cassady et al., 2004; Hansen & Feldhusen, 1994; Johnsen, Haensly, Ryser, & Ford, 2002; VanTassel-Baska et al., 2003). Appendix A contains copies of these highly useful tools.

Teacher perceptions. Identifying teachers' perceptions of the drivers, potential roadblocks, and their own needs and interests with respect to the targeted direction is critical to their participation in professional development and can provide useful insights regarding factors inhibiting change. The most reliable data derive from teachers' analyses of student performance on their curriculum-based assessments (VanTassel-Baska, 2003d). Focus group interviews can shape and refine more formal and larger-scale needs assessment surveys. Appendix B provides (a) a sample needs assessment survey, administered online, that includes items on needs, interests, drivers, and perceived obstacles with respect to Standard 4, Instructional Strategies, and (b) a self-assessment on the 70 knowledge and skill statements of the 10 national standards.

5. *Building collaborations.* Collaborations are important to support professional development, resolve perceived obstacles, and move toward the desired future state. Dettmer et al. (2006) emphasize the importance of involving representatives of intended participants (teachers, administrators, psychologists) as well as other stakeholders (e.g., families and students) in the planning team that will create the professional development plan. Planning for professional development objectives that integrate specializations, such as effective strategies for gifted English language learners, gifted students with disabilities, or rigor in the content areas, benefits from collaboration across district programs. Sample professional development plans for activities involving group audiences (e.g., teachers of advanced courses) can be found in Dettmer et al. (2006) and Dettmer and Landrum (1998). Dettmer and Landrum (1998) also share ideas for incentives for participation, including graduate credits, credit for salary schedule advancement, sabbaticals, stipends, release time through district-supported substitute teachers, and certification renewal.

Figure 4.1 summarizes the steps of needs sensing and needs assessment and how these processes fit into the larger scope of designing and assessing professional development based on standards.

MEETING INDIVIDUAL TEACHER NEEDS

Conscientious teachers who practice lifelong learning pursue professional development as a matter of course through voluntary participation in workshops and conferences. They also engage in informal independent study, for example, when facing a new challenge for which they do not feel adequately prepared (e.g., assignment of new content or new population, such as a gifted student with autism).

Karnes and Shaunessy (2004) describe individual development plans as having emerged as a way to involve teachers in decision making and goal setting. Such plans provide opportunities for learning more about their gifted students' needs and how they learn. Individual plans can encourage teachers to align their projects with district goals and national standards. Planning involves teachers in reflecting on teaching and learning, formulating questions to pursue, defining objectives and activities, implementing the project, documenting accomplishments, assessing effectiveness, and coming back to reflection.

Teachers can incorporate a range of activities in their individual plans (Dettmer et al., 2006; Karnes & Shaunessy, 2004):

- Engaging in individual or small-group inquiry, such as action research, to determine a strategy's effectiveness or solve a common problem
- Seeking consultation and coaching to support application of new skills

Figure 4.1   Identifying Professional Development Objectives Through Needs Sensing and Needs Assessment

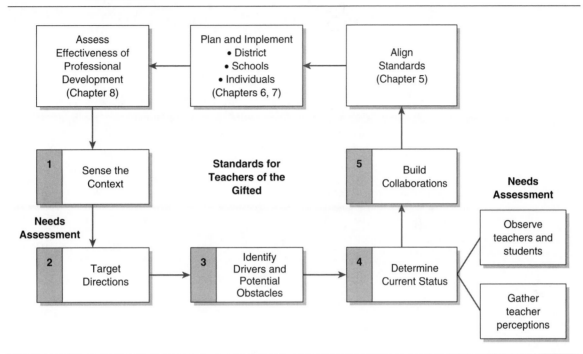

- Attending conferences or workshops
- Taking a course
- Entering and completing a certificate or graduate program
- Joining a study group to read and discuss professional literature
- Reviewing, analyzing, and revising curriculum
- Videotaping one's teaching for small-group review and feedback
- Sharing and discussing student products; evaluating for rigor
- Observing master teachers and how students respond

Karnes and Shaunessy (2004) provide a sample individual professional development plan in gifted education. Based on their work, an example of a standards-based professional development plan for teachers of the gifted and talented appears in Appendix C.

The next chapter provides one approach to identifying district-level professional development outcomes for teachers through alignment of national, state, and local standards for beginning teachers of the gifted, programs for the gifted, and content as well as district demographics, evaluation data, and teacher needs.

5

Identifying Expected Outcomes for Professional Development Through Standards Alignment

Margie Kitano

The processes of needs sensing and assessment (Chapter 4) enable district leaders to identify areas in which teachers would benefit from professional development. Districts also have national, state, and local directives that necessarily influence professional development objectives. This chapter describes one district's process for integrating needs sensing and assessment data with various directives by aligning them to identify specific expected outcomes for teacher development.

The national standards for initial preparation of teachers of the gifted and talented, supported by an extensive research literature, provide guidance for school districts' selection and professional development of teachers. However, the reality is that districts may require teachers of the gifted to address simultaneously a number of different sets of standards. These sets vary, based on the following:

- Categorical services (e.g., gifted and talented, English language learners)
- Content or subject matter (e.g., English language arts, mathematics, science, social sciences, visual and performing arts)
- Focus: standards for teacher knowledge and skills or program standards
- Level of authority: national, state, or district standards

Additionally, individual districts or schools may require or encourage specific approaches to instruction, such as shared and guided reading or writers' workshops. Moreover, teachers vary in training and experience, and professional development must address their identified needs. How can programs for the gifted and talented address the national standards for initial preparation of teachers within this complex context?

One strategy is to examine the alignment of the various sets of standards teachers are asked to consider in working with gifted and talented students in conjunction with their assessed needs. San Diego Unified School District's Gifted and Talented Education (GATE) program offers an example of determining professional development expectations through standards alignment integrated with identified teacher needs. California does not require certification of teachers to work with gifted and talented students beyond the general teacher credential. Current state legislation provides funds to districts with programs approved as meeting California program standards. These standards require that districts receiving funds provide professional development opportunities in gifted education without mandating a specific number of hours. San Diego Unified School District requires that teachers with primary responsibility for working with gifted and talented learners receive a certificate in gifted and talented education through satisfactory completion of a district-provided course or earning of a graduate-level university certificate or master's degree in the field.

The district's certification course is offered collaboratively with San Diego State University. The course team (GATE program manager, program specialists, lead psychologist, and university faculty in gifted education) recently engaged in revising the course. To identify expected outcomes for the certification course, the team examined several sources of information with specific attention to standards alignment. Table 5.1 summarizes the nature of information reviewed and how the various standards and needs data, including results of needs sensing and needs assessment, aligned. The table summarizes information and standards in six key areas:

I. The national NAGC-CEC standards for beginning teachers of the gifted

II. The NAGC PreK–12 Gifted Program Standards, as modified and elaborated on in Landrum, Callahan, and Shaklee (2001)

III. The California state standards for gifted programs

IV. The district's literacy, mathematics, and science curriculum maps, designed to incorporate the California content standards and curriculum framework, with maps identifying essential questions and inquiry units by grade level in each subject area

V. District policies and procedures governing the gifted and talented education program

VI. Local student and teacher needs, as suggested by several indicators derived from needs sensing and assessment processes:
- Results of the district's annual GATE program evaluation of student outcomes. The evaluation provides data on identification and participation rates, outcomes on district and state standardized achievement tests disaggregated by program type; grade level; and ethnic group, English language proficiency, and economic status
- Districtwide meetings of administrators, teachers, and families organized by feeder patterns
- Student and family surveys
- Ongoing teacher evaluations of the district certification course
- Web-based survey of all GATE-certified teachers and administrators in the district
- Walk-through classroom observations conducted by the GATE program manager and district-level curriculum leaders

These data collectively suggested a need for (a) improved identification of and services to gifted students who are English language learners and those from diverse backgrounds, (b) vertical teaming, (c) increased level of rigor and challenge in implementing differentiated instruction, and (d) additional time for novice GATE teachers to observe effective GATE colleagues, practice new differentiation strategies, and receive coaching in implementation.

As indicated by Table 5.1, the alignment of national, state, and local core and gifted program standards and standards for beginning teachers of the gifted as well as district data helped the professional development team identify expected outcomes for district certification in gifted education (last column). The identified knowledge and skill statements map back to the national standards for beginning teachers. References to the specific knowledge and skills statements are shown in parentheses. For brevity, the summary table includes only the general standard statements. Users need to consider the specific items that define each general standard. The San Diego case is only one example of a district's approach to alignment.

Table 5.1   Aligning Standards to Identify District Professional Development Expectations for Teachers

National Standards	State Standards	District Standards	District-Identified Knowledge & Skill Areas for Teachers of the Gifted
Core Examples • National Council for Teachers of Mathematics http://standards.nctm.org • National Council of Teachers of English www.ncte.org/about/over/standards	Example: California content standards and curriculum frameworks for • English language arts • Mathematics • History/Social science • Science • Visual & performing arts • English language development http://www.cde.ca.gov/be/st	**IV.** Example: San Diego Unified's curriculum maps for literacy, mathematics, and science aligned with the California standards. http://www.sandi.net	• Understand the difference between core and differentiated curriculum. (7K2) • Integrate differentiation strategies with District's curriculum maps. (7S1)
I. Standards for Beginning Teachers of the Gifted NAGC/CEC Initial Knowledge & Skill Standards for Gifted and Talented Education	**II. Program Standards** NAGC PreK–12 Gifted Program Standards	**III. State Program Standards** Example: CA State Board of Education Recommended Standards for Programs for Gifted and Talented Students, July 2005 Revision	**V. District GATE Program** www.sandi.net/GATE2/#2	**VI. Considerations** • District demographics • Student achievement outcomes • Walk-through observations • Professional development evaluations • Online survey
1. Foundations Understand the field as an evolving and changing discipline based on philosophies, evidence-based principles and theories, relevant laws and policies, diverse and historical points of view, and human issues . . . understand how issues of human diversity impact	**Program Design** The development of appropriate gifted education programming requires comprehensive services based on sound philosophical, theoretical, and empirical support.	**1. Program Design** Districts provide a comprehensive continuum of services and program options responsive to the needs, interests, and abilities of gifted students and based on philosophical, theoretical, and empirical support.	• **Cluster Program** Provides GATE Cluster-identified students at Grades 3–12 with curricular options that modify depth, complexity, acceleration, and novelty of the core curriculum. • **Seminar Program** Serves GATE Seminar-identified students in Grades 3–12. Modifications of depth,	Understand evidence-based structures and approaches for addressing the needs of gifted students. (1K2)

National Standards	State Standards	District Standards	District-Identified Knowledge & Skill Areas for Teachers of the Gifted
families, cultures, and schools, and how these complex human issues can interact in the delivery of gifted and talented educational services.		complexity, acceleration, and novelty are applied to the core curriculum at levels commensurate with student ability. Restricted to 20 students per classroom in a self-contained, full-day class at the elementary level and selected courses at the secondary level. • Advanced Placement (AP) • International Baccalaureate • College courses	
Program Administration and Management—Appropriate gifted educational programming must include the establishment of a systematic means of developing, implementing, and managing services.	[addressed by 1, 3, 6, 8]	13 full-time employees provide GATE student identification services to all district schools, professional development, and district-level coordination of the GATE program to 146 participating schools.	• Manage the differentiated classroom, using strategies such as compacting, tiering, anchoring, and independent study. (4K2)
Student Identification—Gifted learners must be assessed to determine appropriate educational services.	2. **Identification**—The district's identification procedures are equitable, comprehensive, and ongoing.	Every public school student enrolled within its boundaries shall have the opportunity to take the GATE test in 2nd grade. Students may be retested in Grade 5 or 7.	• Know district assessment procedures and criteria. (8K1) • Preassess learning needs and adjust instruction based on a variety of ongoing curriculum-based assessments to plan instruction and evaluate progress. (4S4)
8. **Assessment**—Use the results of assessments to adjust instruction and to enhance ongoing learning progress . . .			

(Continued)

43

Table 5.1 (Continued)

National Standards	State Standards	District Standards	District-Identified Knowledge & Skill Areas for Teachers of the Gifted
Curriculum and Instruction—Gifted education services must include curricular and instructional opportunities directed to the unique needs of the gifted learner. **4. Instructional strategies**—Possess a repertoire of evidence-based curriculum and instructional strategies to differentiate for individuals with gifts and talents . . . . **5. Learning Environments and Social Interactions**—Actively create learning environments . . . that foster cultural understanding, safety and emotional well-being, positive social interactions, and active engagement . . . foster environments in which diversity is valued . . . . **6. Language and Communication**—Understand the role of language and communication in talent development and the ways in which exceptional conditions can hinder or facilitate such development . . . , match their communication methods to an individual's language proficiency and cultural and linguistic differences . . .	**3. Curriculum and Instruction**—Districts develop differentiated curriculum, instructional models, and strategies that are aligned with and extend to the state academic content standards and curriculum frameworks. The differentiated curriculum is related to theories, models, and practices from the recognized literature in the field.	**Program Goals** • To provide for differentiated opportunities for learning commensurate with abilities and talents of individuals. • To offer alternative learning environments in which students can acquire skills and understandings of advanced ideological and creative levels commensurate with their potential. • To assist in developing self-generating, problem-solving abilities to expand each student's awareness of choices for satisfying contributions in his or her environment.	• Pace instruction consistent with learning needs. (4S5) • Encourage higher-level thinking through strategies such as problem-based learning, inductive strategies, Bloom's taxonomy, and Socratic seminars. (4S2) • Adapt or create a differentiated unit that includes global generalizations, depth and complexity, higher-order thinking, multicultural issues. (4S6) • Encourage and model respect for the full range of diversity among G&T. (9S3) • Apply and share effective strategies for a specific diverse group. (6S1, 7S2,4) • Understand and incorporate rigor and content imperatives in the differentiated curriculum. (7S5) • Teach students to explore, develop, and research

National Standards	State Standards	District Standards	District-Identified Knowledge & Skill Areas for Teachers of the Gifted
7. Instructional Planning—Develop long-range plans anchored in both general and special curricula. . . . take into consideration . . . cultural and linguistic factors.			• their areas of interest or talent, integrating informational technologies. (4S3 & 7) • Teach students the structured methods of inquiry in each discipline. (7S5) • Apply backward planning to ensure access and success in capstone courses. (7S3)
2. Development and Characteristics—Know and demonstrate respect for their students as unique human beings. . . . **3. Individual Learning Differences** – Understand the effects that gifts and talents can have on an individual's learning in school and throughout life . . . active and resourceful in seeking to understand how language, culture, and family background interact . . .	**Socioemotional Guidance and Counseling**—Gifted education programming must establish a plan to recognize and nurture the unique socioemotional development of gifted learners. **4. Social and Emotional Development**—Districts establish and implement plans to support the social and emotional development of gifted learners to increase responsibility, self-awareness, and other issues of affective development.	**Program Goals** • To help gifted and talented students develop sensitivity and responsibility to others. • To help develop a commitment in gifted and talented students to constructive ethical standards. • To develop realistic healthy self-concepts.	• Understand differences and similarities within gifted population. (2K5) • Understand the influence of culture, socioeconomic status, language, and dual exceptionality on the development of gifted students. (3K1) • Understand, empathize, and appreciate cognitive and social/emotional needs and implications for curriculum and instruction. (3K2)
9. Professional and Ethical Practice—Are guided by the profession's ethical and professional practice standards . . . understand that culture and language interact with gifts and	**Professional Development**—Gifted learners are entitled to be served by professionals who have specialized preparation in gifted education, expertise in appropriate differentiated **5. Professional Development**—Districts provide professional development opportunities related to gifted education to administrators, teachers, and staff to support and improve	District requires GATE certification for all GATE Seminar and GATE Cluster teachers. Options: District GATE certificate, graduate certificate in gifted education from an accredited university,	• Assess own current knowledge and skill levels. (9S1) • Complete an in-depth independent study with a contract in one GATE area of interest. (9S5)

(Continued)

Table 5.1 (Continued)

National Standards	State Standards	District Standards	District-Identified Knowledge & Skill Areas for Teachers of the Gifted
talents and are sensitive to the many aspects of diversity of individuals with gifts and talents and their families.	content and instructional methods, and involvement in ongoing professional development and who possess exemplary personal and professional traits. educational opportunities for gifted students.	or a master's degree in gifted education. District certification offered through collaboration with local university, equivalent to three semester units. GATE office also sponsors • Courses for district credit • Distinguished lecture series	
10. Collaboration— Effectively collaborate with families, other educators, and related service providers . . . promote and advocate for the learning and well-being of individuals with gifts and talents across settings and diverse learning experiences.	6. Parent and Community Involvement—Districts provide procedures to ensure consistent participation of parents and community members in the planning and evaluation of programs for gifted students.	• Meetings for parents of identified GATE students • Cluster Review Task Force • Seminar Task Force • GATE District Advisory Committee • Program Governance Team • Vertical teams	Have techniques and resources for working with GATE parents. (10K1)
Program Evaluation— Program evaluation is the systematic study of the value and impact of services provided.	7. Program Assessment— Districts establish formal and informal evaluation methods and instruments that assess the gifted program and the performance of gifted students (which meets or exceeds state content standards). Results of data collected, including state standardized tests, are used	Conducted annually by District Program Studies Department. Provides demographics and comparisons of identified GATE students who participate and who do not participate in gifted programs on state standardized achievement and district tests.	Understand what to look for in assessing the effectiveness of a GATE classroom (cluster and seminar).

National Standards	State Standards	District Standards	District-Identified Knowledge & Skill Areas for Teachers of the Gifted
	to study the value and impact of the services provided and to improve gifted programs and gifted student performance.	Parent/student surveys	
	8. **Budgets**—District budgets for gifted programs support and provide for all the components of the district's GATE program and meet the related standards.	District supplements state funding with substantial district funds.	

6

An Effective, Standards-Based Professional Development Model for Gifted Education

Joyce VanTassel-Baska

The importance of professional development in the world of PreK–12 schools is at an all-time high for several reasons. First, it continues to be the primary methodology through which teachers update their skills and new teachers are socialized to the priorities of a particular school and/or district. Second, professional development is the major mechanism for implementing the curriculum reform of recent state standards and assessment practices. Finally, in an age of teacher shortages and concomitant alternative licensure programs, all schools must have a sufficiently broad professional development thrust to prepare novitiates to education "on the job." Because of the priority of these three agendas, it is difficult to focus on the needs of gifted learners as an emphasis for school districts in their professional development planning.

Yet new developments in gifted education have presaged the need for strong attention to this component of program development. The October 2006 passage of new National Council for Accreditation of Teacher Education (NCATE) standards for gifted education provides an important umbrella for all professional development activities in the field. By emphasizing the major knowledge and skills necessary for teachers to work effectively with this population, the new standards provide an important avenue for coherent work with the following populations of educational personnel: (a) regular classroom teachers who will not take an endorsement or certificate in gifted education, (b) administrators who have program responsibility for gifted education but lack the background, and (c) endorsed or certified teachers of the gifted who want to go deeper into work in one or more of the 10 standards.

Moreover, many current models of delivery in gifted education involve regular classroom teachers to a great extent, either as sole providers or as partners or collaborators with specially trained teachers of the gifted (Kirschenbaum, Armstrong, & Landrum, 1999; Tomlinson, 2001). In addition, cluster grouping in the regular classroom has become an equally viable option to pullout programs in many locales (Winebrenner, 1994).

All these situations suggest the need for more professional development, especially for regular classroom teachers, in working with gifted learners. Current research and evaluation data also have continued to suggest that regular classroom teachers are ill prepared to differentiate for curriculum and instruction of gifted students in the regular classroom to any extent (Avery, VanTassel-Baska, & O'Neill, 1997; Westberg, Archambault, Dobyns, & Slavin, 1993; Westberg & Daoust, 2003). This chapter describes a workable, research-based professional development model from needs assessment to evaluation that incorporates the standards for teachers of the gifted.

ELEMENTS OF EFFECTIVE PROFESSIONAL DEVELOPMENT

While the agenda for professional development needs continues to grow with some urgency in general education and gifted education, research on effective teaching (Wenglinsky, 2000), evaluation of staff development models (Kennedy, 1999), and research on staff development practices (Guskey, 2000) provide important blueprints for developing effective contemporary staff development programs. Garet, Porter, Desimone, Birman, and Yoon (2001) summarized the research-based features of professional development that significantly impact classroom practice. These features include the following:

1. *A strong focus on content knowledge.* Echoed also by Kennedy's (1999) research that relates to the importance of embedding professional development work in content, this feature suggests the need for strategies to be directly applied by the facilitator to specific content to be taught.

2. *Opportunities for active learning.* All effective professional development sessions must allow time for participant interaction on problems, issues, and learning applications.

3. *Coherence with other learning activities.* Professional development sessions must show alignment to other teacher activities and needs. For example, gifted workshops should routinely show how the skill or strategy relates to the relevant state standards for learning and how it relates to hallmark secondary programs such as Advanced Placement.

4. *Sustained intensive opportunities.* Professional development must employ more than isolated workshops or the choice of conference sessions. It must be planned in an acceptable mode, delivered effectively, followed up, and assessed by student impact measures.

5. *Collective participation.* No longer can professional developers be satisfied with a few people "buying in" to a set of practices. There is a need to engage all teachers, principals, and central office staff in the relevant changes to be made.

APPLICATIONS TO GIFTED EDUCATION

Since the bulk of professional development research has been done at a generic level in respect to all educators, perhaps it is useful to consider what needs to be tailored for teachers and administrators working with gifted populations, linked to the NCATE standards. Obviously, the content needs to be modified to focus more sharply on differentiation strategies, flexible classroom grouping strategies, and alternative assessment protocols. Moreover, the processes of delivery need to be carefully considered. Can professional development for the gifted be successfully combined with other topics? Should all teachers be held to state endorsement or certification standards in gifted education? What combination of professional development approaches would be most effective in an annual plan? These questions are central to designing an effective professional development model for gifted education.

Using the Guskey (2000) model for evaluating professional development practices as a design for planning, the following questions need to be asked:

1. What knowledge and skills should educators acquire about gifted students and their learning? This question is now answered by the new standards in 10 core areas.

2. Under what delivery mode will the educators best acquire these understandings (e.g., study groups, workshops, action research, mentoring)? This question is a local one, to be decided in context.

3. What organizational support structures are in place to facilitate change?
   a. Are adequate resources available for classroom implementation?
   b. Will implementation be monitored? How?
   c. Is the climate supportive of experimentation?

4. How will program coordinators assess the application of the knowledge and skills acquired?

5. What was the impact on gifted students of educators' acquiring new knowledge and skills?

There are several pragmatic problems in planning effective professional development in gifted education related to resources and leadership. Because of limited funding for professional development in many locales and the pressing needs of general education, sources of "fair share" apportioned funding from general staff development coffers have been reduced or eliminated. Reductions in gifted education budgets have also impacted on effective planning in this area. The basic allocations for hiring staff and purchasing materials for classrooms clearly supersede professional development budget considerations. Moreover, availability of teachers for staff development has become more limited as part of the cost is in release time where substitutes must be paid or in direct stipends to teachers for extra time expended. Only so much time can be available, and the use of that time has to be prioritized, leading to gifted education's potentially being left out of the equation.

Another problem that affects professional development planning in this area is the lack of prepared leadership in schools. Some program coordinators are not prepared in gifted education themselves and so lack the capacity to plan effective opportunities or to prepare others. Other coordinators have not internalized the new paradigms of professional development that focus on enhanced student learning as the real test of effective staff development programs and so continue to offer discrete inservice workshops and conference attendance with no follow-up as their approach.

GUIDELINES AND STEPS FOR STANDARDS-BASED PROFESSIONAL DEVELOPMENT

As educators of the gifted consider the demands for time and resources in current school climates, they may wish to adopt the following professional development suggestions in incorporating the new NCATE standards *annually* into their planning:

1. Target four workshops for all teachers on working with gifted students; target four advanced workshops for teachers specializing in gifted education, and target two abbreviated (2–3 hours) workshops for building and central office administrators.

2. Establish content priorities for workshops based on program needs, not individual teacher desires. Conduct a needs assessment or use recent evaluation data to determine those program needs. Link program needs to the relevant standards in gifted education for development of workshop content emphases. Use the NCATE evidence base of annotations (Chapter 2) to create a resource list of readings for teachers, emphasizing the relevant entries from research, literature, and practice sections.

3. Provide follow-up support in each building to ensure that teachers can implement new skills. Provide relevant book and print resources, discuss the plan for implementation with each principal, visit classrooms to "get the feel" for teacher issues, and attend a faculty meeting in the building to judge climates.

4. Develop a system of monitoring implementation of professional development work. Visit a few classrooms each week with a checklist of target teacher behaviors (see Appendix A). Discuss observations with teachers. Ask principals to visit classrooms regularly and look for these same instructional behaviors. Work with teacher teams to develop self-monitoring strategies for implementing new strategies.

5. Assess impact of professional development work on gifted students through questionnaires, test scores, and/or structured interviews with students and parents.

6. Develop one-year and three-year plans for professional development activities that reflect a compelling vision for improvement based on needs assessment and/or evaluation data collected. Districts lacking improvement plans or needs assessment data can use the standards for entry-level teachers of the gifted as a base to consider what needs to be done. A sample plan appears in Table 6.1, including goal, desired outcome, mode of delivery, support strategy, and assessment approach.

7. Develop a collaborative relationship with a university-based center in gifted education to tap into important resources and cost-effective professional development opportunities.

8. Be deliberate about all phases of professional development from planning to implementation through follow-up and assessment. Conducting workshops is only the beginning of the effort.

By incorporating a strong professional development model in the district, program improvements in curriculum, instruction, assessment, communication, and parental involvement should begin to occur. This alone constitutes a reason to implement it!

Table 6.1   Sample Professional Development Plan

Identified need: All teachers need better-developed skills in teaching critical thinking as one of the five goals in our gifted program (linked to NCATE Standard 4 on Instructional Strategies).

Evidence for need: Evaluation report in 2000; needs assessment with gifted teacher specialists in 2001. Research-based evidence in NCATE Standard 4.

2007–2008 goals for professional development:

1. To provide a series of four workshops for all teachers on Richard Paul's (Elder & Paul, 2003) model of reasoning, emphasizing the elements of issue, purpose, concept, assumptions, point of view, inference, and consequences and implications.

2. To provide an abbreviated two-workshop model for principals that gives an overview of the model and follow-up strategies.

Desired outcome: Evidence of using the reasoning model will be displayed in 80% of classrooms monitored in schools participating; gifted students and parents reflect a positive attitude about the new emphasis on higher-level thinking; student achievement on performance measures demonstrates enhanced learning in this area.

Mode of delivery: Workshop series

Support strategy: All teachers and schools trained will receive materials describing the use of the model, accompanied by sample lesson plans for each core subject area and relevant grade levels.

Assessment approach: (a) Assessment of teacher implementation will be completed via observation by June 2008, (b) student assessment of attitudes via questionnaire by June 2008, (c) student product and/or performance assessment by June 2008.

CONCLUSION

Professional development programs geared to address the differentiated learning needs of gifted learners must be carefully planned and executed with a clear vision of the current educational context and research-based best practices articulated in the new NAGC-CEC standards in gifted education. Older staff development options offering episodic instruction must give way to more sophisticated long-term intensive efforts if gifted education is to remain a viable part of education program structures in schools. These new standards provide a clear blueprint for that to happen.

7

Designing Professional Development Activities at Teacher and School Levels

Diane Montgomery

Every school will have children and youth who are gifted and will require teachers who possess the knowledge and skills to teach gifted learners from all backgrounds. Designing professional development to incorporate the national standards requires thoughtful planning and substantial effort on the part of participating teachers and other school personnel. Teachers invest time in prioritizing their needs (see Chapter 4) in the context of the school, community, and student characteristics. Each activity, technique, method, or strategy must be congruent with the overall goal, mission, or strategy of the school and its teachers. Services to gifted and talented children and youth can improve by engaging teachers in standards-based professional development—one teacher or one school at a time. While the standards drive the content of the plan, the path to successful professional development may vary for each teacher and school. The forgoing chapter described a model for effective district-level planning and designing of standards-based professional development in gifted education. This chapter offers ideas for professional development at the individual and school level with techniques and models for constructing personal professional development plans (Dettmer & Landrum, 1998; Karnes & Shaunessy, 2004) and school plans involving collaboration and coaching.

PRINCIPLES OF PROFESSIONAL DEVELOPMENT: THE INDIVIDUAL

Thomas Guskey's (1991, 2003b) broadly accepted guidelines for quality professional development begin with what teachers each intuitively know: Change occurs at the individual level, one professional at a time. There are three principles to recognize when planning for teacher change: Teacher change (a) requires effort, (b) occurs over long periods of time, and (c) benefits from conscious planning and support with resources. These principles from Guskey's research suggest that school change needs to be planned incrementally, at the teacher level. Clearly, it is not possible for all teachers to demonstrate the 70 or more knowledge and skills listed in the 10 standards for teacher preparation in gifted education within one year or even within three or more years. However, starting with one standard and growing gradually and incrementally can result in major changes in services provided to gifted students. Guskey emphasizes the importance of working in teams and integrating procedures to garner feedback on the instructional changes that school personnel identified as necessary. Support and follow-up are essential features of every professional development program.

Professional development activities may be the charge of one designated professional, a schoolwide team, or a districtwide committee. This person or team is responsible for assessing needs, planning approaches to meet the needs, and evaluating effectiveness of the implemented plan. The model for professional development may emphasize the environment of one specific school as the *context* for teacher learning. Because change begins with teachers in their classrooms, the district can promote implementation of the standards by supporting the individual or team responsible for coordinating individual plans that teachers construct within the schools.

Starting at the individual level, offering a broad list of options to teachers such as those in Table 7.1 allows each person to find what suits his or her own learning style and motivation rather than requiring everyone to experience the same activity. The options are various activities that can support any content area toward any standard. It is important to coordinate planning so that the activities fit together to meet the goals for the school. For our purposes, the standards dominate the planning for each method.

Many veteran teachers of the gifted are most interested in starting with knowledge and skills related to teaching and curriculum, which include Standards 4 (Instructional Strategies) and 7 (Instructional Planning). Teachers who have never worked with gifted learners may have interest in learning about gifted students themselves (Standards 2, Development and Characteristics of Learners, and 3, Individual Learning Differences) and how they are identified (Standard 8, Assessment). The steps for personal professional development plans are as follows:

- Step 1: Make a personal commitment to work on the standards.
- Step 2: Start with one standard of great interest or self-diagnosed need.
- Step 3: Pick from Table 7.1 something that can be immediately implemented.
- Step 4: Get help in assessing the extent to which you have progressed.

Table 7.1   School-Based Professional Development Strategies

- Reading groups (book club, journal reviews, etc.)
- Observation of other teachers
- Mentoring or shadowing other teachers
- Teacher-led seminars
- Team teaching
- Classroom coaching
- Local teacher networks (including other schools in the district or nearby)
- Collaborative curriculum planning
- Action research project
- Formalized feedback from teams or master teachers
- Taking responsibilities of master teachers (curriculum, mentoring, etc.)
- Leadership or member involvement in professional associations
- Reflective practice sessions with peers
- Inviting external providers to deliver seminars, symposiums, and workshops

Table 7.2 provides sample professional development activities. Standards addressed by each activity appear in parentheses. Table 7.3 presents a sample school professional development plan that assists with connecting individual teacher development needs within a schoolwide professional development plan. The priority comes from the standards identified in the needs assessment by each individual teacher. The strategy is a combination of activities or methods to address the priority. Specifying the schedule, personnel responsible, and outcomes will assist planners in ensuring progress for teachers at the school level each year.

COACHING MODELS FOR PROFESSIONAL DEVELOPMENT

Effective models of professional development for teachers of the gifted typically include coaching and mentoring by consultant teachers who guide implementation of standards in practice. Coaching and mentoring are models proposed by many, particularly professional organizations, as necessary components to a complete professional development program (International Reading Association & National Association for the Education of Young Children, 1998; Landry, Swank, Smith, Assel, & Gunnewig, 2006). In these models, a master teacher serves in a peer, not supervisory, role with teachers who have common goals. Coaches and mentors would be particularly helpful in the areas of curriculum planning (Standard 7), instructional practices (Standard 4), social and emotional needs of students (Standards 2, 3, and 5), collaboration with colleagues (Standard 10), and assessment tools (Standard 8).

Peer coaching to support teachers' implementation of a newly learned instructional strategy typically includes three phases: planning, observing, and processing.

Table 7.2 Sample Professional Development Activities

Professional Development Strategy	Activity
Observation of other teachers	Visit a classroom or gifted program that has students from diverse backgrounds this teaching period and reflect how it relates to my work. (3K1, 9S7)
Mentoring or shadowing other teachers	Arrange to demonstrate to two other teachers the teaching strategies for questioning learned in my college class. (4K2, 10S4)
Teacher-led seminars	Conduct a six-week series on differentiated curriculum with colleagues on Wednesdays. (10S4)
Team teaching	Propose to administration a trial team-teaching model with two other teachers in order to differentiate curriculum. (7S2)
Classroom coaching	Invite another teacher of the gifted to come to my classroom and coach me for instructional strategies that honor all cultures in my classroom. (5S4, 10S6)
Local teacher networks (including other schools in the district or nearby)	Start a regional gifted educator network to share research-based materials and ideas and meet at least once a month to better identify and serve gifted children from low-income families. (7S4, 9S5)
Collaborative curriculum planning	Coordinate teachers in my area to formally map and evaluate curriculum to determine most appropriate acceleration strategies. (4S5, 7S3)
Action research project	Collaborate with a colleague at the university to describe the school climate for advancing achievement. (10S2)
Formalized feedback from teams or master teachers	Seek feedback from special education colleagues on progress I am making with my gifted student with autism. (3K2, 4K2, 10S6)
Leadership or member involvement in professional associations	Volunteer to be program chair for the state association for gifted yearly conference. (9S6)
Taking responsibilities of master teachers (curriculum, mentoring, etc.)	Initiate a new curriculum committee to investigate ways to assist all teachers in differentiating math and reading. (4K1)
Reflective practice sessions with peers	Participate with three colleagues in meetings on Tuesdays after school to discuss teaching practices. We will start with K & S in Standard 10. (9S7)
Inviting external providers to deliver seminars, symposiums, workshops	Serve on the committee to invite curriculum experts to assist with differentiation strategies for all classrooms. (4K1)

The teacher plans for the coaching by providing a lesson plan using the strategy and identifying the lesson's objectives. The coach inquires about the role he or she should play, what to watch for, and where to locate himself or herself in the classroom. The role might be to observe the teacher's implementation, step in to model, or assist the students. The coach observes the implementation, recording effective aspects and student behaviors consistent with the teachers' requests. The teacher reflects with the coach about the lesson, the coach shares observations, and together they determine next steps.

In gifted education, the consultant model has been identified as an effective method for providing services for gifted students (Hertzog, 1998; Landrum, 2001).

Table 7.3   Sample School Professional Development Plan

Priority	PD Strategy	Schedule	Person Responsible	Resources Needed	Expected Outcome
Standard 4S5: Pace delivery of curriculum and instruction consistent with needs of individuals with gifts and talents.	From Table 6.2, Collaborative Curriculum Planning: Coordinate with peers to map curriculum to support acceleration.	Tuesdays at 3:00 p.m.	Teacher of the gifted who serves as site team leader for gifted program.	Consulting on appropriate assessments for determining students' pacing needs.	Teachers gain skills to appropriately pace curriculum and strategies for accelerating content. Students receive opportunities for pacing and move through the curriculum at a faster rate.

The consultant is a master teacher who may coach, demonstrate strategies, or share expertise through workshops, readings, and materials on topics of common interest. Two variations of the consultant model are the Dynamic Scaffolding Model (Matthews & Foster, 2005) and the Systematic Target to Access Resources (STAR) Model (Montgomery, Otto, & Hull, 2007).

The Dynamic Scaffolding Model (Matthews & Foster, 2005) adapted the general education consultant model for teacher development in gifted education. The gifted consultant works with teachers to meet the needs of students by sharing expertise, materials, and resources. In this program, the consultant does not work with students directly but, rather, provides teachers with "the necessary expertise for dealing with all of their diversely gifted learners" (p. 225) through scaffolding with technical assistance, feedback, and professional development opportunities. The consultant offers workshops, ongoing support for implementation of new practices, and follow-up activities. For example, assessment of professional development may require teachers to implement in their classrooms, within a specific time period, one or more of the learning strategies presented at a workshop. The consultant is available to assist implementation, review teachers' written reflections, and provide follow-up consultation.

The STAR coaching model was developed for the Connecting Community Resources Encouraging All Teachers to Educate with Spirit (CREATES) Project (Montgomery et al., 2007). CREATES is an arts integration and talent development program that uses arts resource coaches to work with teachers, arts educators, and community artists to infuse the arts in adaptations and differentiated curriculum leading to talent development. Project CREATES is conducted in Tulsa, Oklahoma, public schools with students who are from diverse backgrounds and at risk for underachievement. STAR advocates professional development as cocreation, a process for collaboration that occurs when the products (curriculum, lesson, materials, etc.) are owned by all individuals involved in the collaboration. The vernacular used to understand the process is that no one is the boss and everyone is first author. The five points on a star (Figure 7.1) represent categories of some of the strategies provided in Table 7.1 and are described as follows:

1. Cocreation using external resources (field trips to other schools, conferences, speakers)

2. Cocreation using internal resources (consultation, book groups, reflective study groups, individual and small-group inquiry/action research)

3. Cocreation with seminars across schools (using internal or external resources)

4. Cocreation with collaborative planning within school (team planning, grade-level planning, talent group planning)

5. Cocreation with teaching artists to include a minimum of three sessions (coplanning, coteaching, coreflection)

Figure 7.1   Specific Target Actions for Renewal Model

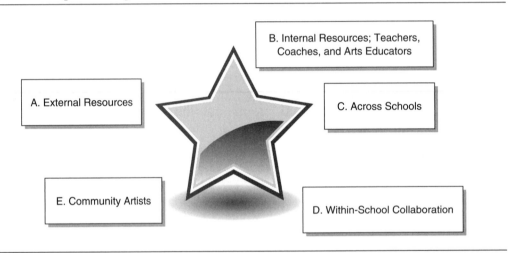

Coaching and consulting are dynamic ways to respond to teachers' changing needs and to maximize the collegial relationships effective in professional development (Dettmer & Landrum, 1998).

8

Assessment of Professional Development Activities

Diane Montgomery

There was a time when professional development for teachers in PreK–12 schools was considered to be primarily the "inservice" workshop, lecture, or seminar led by a motivating outside speaker for the entire school or district staff. Teachers met in the largest space in the school and acted as an audience to receive the new information transmitted by the speaker. While the professional development goal was to change classroom practices, little assessment occurred to discover if any changes were made in classrooms. A survey form completed by each participant constituted the sole evaluation of this large-group lecture given by the external consultant as a professional development activity. The survey may have inquired about whether the goals of the session were met, participants' perceptions of the speaker's knowledge and preparedness, applicability of the content, and quality of the environment. Some forms may have asked if other information was needed to implement the content and invited participants to rate aspects of the venue (e.g., room temperature and food quality). The evaluation results became part of a report to the district or were given to the speaker as feedback on his or her performance before the audience.

The dominance of this method evolved to the point that *inservice* was used as a verb. Administrators might say they were going to "in-service teachers" (Sharma,

1986, p. 4) on a certain topic or instructional strategy to change teaching practices or improve student learning. Although this strategy is still used today, it has become only one piece of a larger professional development plan for the district, schools, and individual professionals. As we experience an expanded range of approaches for delivering professional development, we also see an expanded array of assessment strategies available to determine progress toward our goals.

Assessment of professional development may be conducted on an individual basis, although gifted educators most likely will be interested in schoolwide knowledge of gifted students (e.g., indicators for Standard 10, Collaboration, may be sought). From what we know and have experienced, most classroom teachers across the United States do not receive adequate professional development regarding gifted education. This means that educators of the gifted have a dual focus of advancing their own growth related to the standards, and at the same time, part of their assignment may be to promote development of their faculty colleagues. The gifted educator must by the nature of the situation become the one to help teachers determine which of the standards are most critical for them to demonstrate.

In an analysis of the research used to establish effective professional development, Guskey (2003a) noted that few studies linked the characteristics of effectiveness to specific measures of student improvement in learning. When studies were found to be directly concerned with student outcomes, the measure usually focused on student achievement test scores in a content area. Several researchers have indicated problems associated with yearly student test scores as a measure of any change in teacher behaviors (Kennedy, 1999; Noyce, 2006). Yet teaching effectiveness and student learning can be connected to professional development goals (Fishman, Marx, Best, & Tal, 2003). Guskey (2007) found that school administrators differ from teachers in what they believe indicates student learning. Teachers value classroom observations, homework, and quality of work. In contrast, administrators tend to value standardized national tests of achievement. Gifted students' achievement test scores as a measure of teacher growth must be interpreted within the context of additional complex intervening and co-occurring contributing factors. We need more direct strategies to link teacher growth and student learning.

Effective assessment strategies provide information on ways to adapt the activities or professional development program to meet the individual and school goals related to the standards. Over half the standards relate to issues of diversity that can be targeted for the school. Likely only a few school personnel will identify as an educator of gifted students and establish meeting all the standards as an individual professional goal. Yet when professional development is evaluated as a planned program, it is inclusive of feedback and results from many individual activities. This multidimensional process includes all planned activities, from readiness, practice and coaching to follow-up and support (Guskey & Sparks, 1991). When the goals are stated in terms of student learning outcome, the evaluation process becomes more complex. Instructional strategies and student learning are parts of the whole assessment for acquisition of teacher knowledge and skills.

We did not find many models that include professional standards in the planning or assessment process. Perhaps the field of gifted education may lead the effort to document effectiveness of professional development by using multiple strategies to connect standards mastery with assessment of teacher instructional strategies and student learning outcomes. We should also pursue community resources as another connection. As assessment of teacher professional development progresses on an individual level, connecting to community or parent resources (Public Education Network, 2005) not only addresses the standards for collaboration (Standard 10) but will enhance school climate and culture for assisting teachers in attaining their goals.

One assessment method that holds promise for gifted education is the school-embedded professional development model to improve learning for all children (Parrett, 2005). In this approach, teachers have regular weekly meetings to "collaborate and use assessment data to guide professional decisions" (p. 28). Systems for assessing novice and veteran teacher growth related to student learning (Howard, 2005) incorporate performance dimensions that can be adapted to reflect specific knowledge and skills standards. In the Teacher Growth and Assessment Process system (Howard, 2005), there are self-directed activities for formative evaluation and supervised observations for summative evaluation. The purpose of the system is to identify specific strategies for each teacher's professional development plan.

Assessment approaches that connect the standards to teaching behaviors include self-evaluation, teacher peer feedback, coaching and mentorship model evaluations, concept mapping for teachers, and collaborative teaming for evaluation of curriculum plans or student work. Strategies for gathering evidence of standards implementation related to student learning include authentic assessment of students, observation of student engagement and student efficacy, and student product evaluation.

TEACHER INDICATORS

Self-Evaluation

Regular use of the needs assessment instrument (Appendix B: Sample Needs Assessment Survey) allows self-rating of the level of need for each knowledge and skill in all 10 standards. Keeping a personal record of yearly evaluations supports monitoring of changes in teacher self-perceptions of knowledge and actions. These data might be linked to professional development activities for individual teachers. For example, schools might keep track of the teachers who attended each session offered during professional development days, noting the standard that was the focus of the session and teachers' evaluations of knowledge and skills. They can assist teachers in fulfilling their personal plan of observing other teachers in the building or going out of the district to mentor or shadow other teachers of the gifted. Time is needed to review the information that was tracked in order to make changes.

As teachers of the gifted become more aware of the standards for teacher preparation, they might choose to monitor their own teaching, including planning for student learning (Standards 4, 7, 8). Examples of classroom observations using audio- or videotape to monitor questioning strategies to promote higher levels of thought in student discussion are provided in Schiever's (1991) thorough description and suggested lesson plans for learning the Hilda Taba teaching strategies (Standard 7). A more recent assessment instrument for rating self-behavior can be found in the article by Hong, Greene, and Higgins (2006). Called the Instructional Practice Questionnaire, the areas of assessment relate to cognitive, interpersonal, and intrapersonal aspects of student learning. This instrument gives the teacher ideas about areas related to the standards that can be focus goals for the personal plan.

Peer Feedback, Coaching, and Mentorship

Another strategy to tie the standards to professional development is to arrange for collaboration with other educators. Having a coach observe work with students over a period of time requires time and commitment from both educators. Often the teacher of the gifted may be the only educator working on the standards in gifted education. Requesting another teacher to provide feedback on instructional strategies (Standard 7) or aspects of professionalism (Standard 9) assists the teacher in assessment of areas of growth. Teachers of gifted learners might videotape their own teaching behaviors and demonstrate the techniques of self-assessment in their observation of other classrooms.

An instrument that assists with classroom observations will center the attention on standards related to instructional strategies and student learning. VanTassel-Baska et al. (2003) developed the Classroom Observation Scale-Revised (COS-R), an instrument designed to assess what teachers are doing in the classroom to meet the needs of gifted learners. There are six scales for teachers to use in evaluating their teaching behaviors. The scales were derived from best practices in gifted education (skills in Standard 4) and are curriculum planning and delivery, differentiated teaching behaviors, accommodations for individual differences, problem solving, critical thinking strategies, creative thinking strategies, and research strategies. This instrument (Appendix A) has reliability and validity as a method for assessing teacher change as a result of professional development (VanTassel-Baska, Quek, & Feng, 2007).

The consultant model of professional development discussed in the previous chapter may include workshops on specific standards, with teachers developing lessons that incorporate the new information. The consultant reviews the lesson plans, may observe and coach implementation, require written reflection, and provide feedback and advice on next steps. In this model, rubrics connecting the lesson to specific standards and quality criteria provide assessment data on both strategy implementation by the teacher and the efficacy of consultant support. Appendix D contains one example of a rubric assessing a multicultural literature unit related to specific standards.

Concept Mapping for Teachers

Concept mapping is a strategy that gifted educators may use regularly with students. Given a general concept or focus term, the learner demonstrates his or her own understanding by adding ideas to elaborate or define the central concept and by drawing lines between ideas to indicate connections. The line might have a verb or preposition to denote the relationship between ideas. Often, concepts are interrelated and the lines cross over to another concept coming from the main focus term. Each level of concept can be scored for relevance to the focus term, accuracy, and nonredundancy among all ideas presented in the map. Changes in knowledge can be easily identified by the individual or scored to monitor growth patterns of a group of learners. Johnsen and Pennington (2005) used concept mapping as a pre/postassessment to quantitatively document changes in preservice teachers' perceptions regarding gifted student growth and development. Appendix E provides an example of pre/postchanges in one teacher's understanding of "effective teaching strategies for gifted and talented students." The appendix includes instructions for developing the concept map and for scoring results. Using Johnsen and Pennington's model, professional development personnel can monitor changes in teachers' understanding of concepts required by the standards, such as curriculum differentiation. Omission of the same critical idea by several teachers may indicate a need for professional development in that area.

Collaborative Work Teams

Other national professional organizations have standards for teachers who work in specific content areas. National standards usually have major emphases in the area of assessment, which holds true for gifted educators as well. Standard 8 for teacher preparation in gifted education has four skills and three areas of knowledge. As teachers plan collaborative work teams to analyze student work (Krebs, 2005), they learn how to integrate standards in their teaching process (Parrett, 2005). Teachers use student assessment results to modify instruction based on the standards and their own goals for professional development. Research has identified planning and reflection time as administrative supports necessary in teacher work teams.

STUDENT INDICATORS

Authentic Assessment

Instruments chosen to assess students must be linked to the intervention that the teacher or schools targeted for professional development. For example, if the focus for teacher change is to encourage greater creative expression in the classroom, then student products can be assessed for creative expression. Some examples are student portfolios, criterion-referenced tests in specific content areas, professional expert opinion, rubrics, and classroom interaction analysis.

Student Engagement

When specific learning needs are met, students demonstrate high levels of motivation. Taking attendance, monitoring tardiness, and assessing time on task can provide one type of data to assess level of student motivation to attend school. Additionally, gifted students might report their involvement at home or on weekends for specialized research projects if Standard 4, Skill 3 is a priority for the teacher (provide opportunities for individuals with gifts and talents to explore, develop, or research their areas of interest or talent). There is evidence that certain types of professional development can enhance student engagement. Using general and Title I school classrooms, Stichter, Lewis, Richter, Johnson, and Bradley (2006) found that teachers who used peer coaching were better at providing opportunities for students to respond to questions and prompts. The amount and type of student response was increased when teachers made a conscious effort to encourage student participation and thinking. Three of the observation instruments in Appendix A, developed for use with gifted students, include ratings on student engagement in general or on specific types of differentiated activities.

Student Efficacy

Teachers of the gifted are expected to know the affective characteristics of students in Standards 2 and 3 and develop skills to respond to such needs in

Standard 5. At the same time, gifted students feel different about themselves based on their frame of reference—the general classroom or the gifted program option. Ensuring a positive learning environment may include the assessment of student opinions about self. Instruments measuring esteem, multiple dimensions of self-concept, and belief in self-abilities (efficacy) are available to document changes in student opinions as changes in the school and class climate are enacted.

Student Product Evaluation

Student products are often scored using a rubric. Validity is supported by expert consensus that the rubrics accurately assess the extent to which products meet the evaluation criteria. Reliability of the rubric is increased when multiple raters give the same scores to the same product. Working in teaching teams, teachers of the gifted might begin to build evidence of the standards in student rubrics. For example, teachers of the gifted might collaborate (Standard 10) with general classroom teachers to extend rubrics used with all students to include the challenge and complexity necessary for gifted learners. The Reis and Renzulli (1991) Student Product Assessment Form is one example of a valid and reliable instrument to aid teachers in evaluating students' creative products.

There is much work to be done in gifted education to learn how to plan and evaluate professional development based on student and teacher learning as they relate to the standards for teachers of the gifted. Integrating the standards into professional plans and identifying strategies for assessing growth constitute important first steps.

9

Professional Development and the Diversity Standards

Margie Kitano

I n 2000, the Council for Exceptional Children (CEC) added multicultural standards (CEC, 2005) to the common core governing preparation of teachers of students with special needs, including the gifted and talented. The NAGC-CEC's revised national standards for entry-level teachers of the gifted retain this emphasis in the standards. All knowledge and skill statements apply to working with all gifted and talented students, including those from backgrounds diverse by ethnicity, culture, economic status, language, ability/disability, and sexual orientation. Additionally, specific language in the standards and many knowledge and skill statements make clear reference to diverse populations. This chapter begins with a summary of diversity knowledge, skills, and dispositions expected of beginning teachers of the gifted and describes the rationale for this focus as well as approaches and strategies for addressing diversity standards in PreK–12 professional development.

SUMMARY OF STANDARDS SPECIFIC TO DIVERSITY

Within the 10 national standards for beginning teachers of the gifted, 27 of the 70 knowledge and skill statements contain specific reference to diversity, and an additional 4 to assistive technologies and other needs of gifted students with disabilities.

Table 9.1 highlights in narrative format what entry-level teachers of the gifted should know and be able to do with respect to gifted students from diverse backgrounds and their families.

RATIONALE

Data on gifted and talented learners disaggregated by group as well as growing literature in the field argue the need for educators of the gifted and talented to possess specific knowledge and skills with respect to diversity.

1. *Continued underrepresentation.* African American and Latino students, English language learners, and students with disabilities continue to be underrepresented in programs for the gifted. U.S. Office of Civil Rights data projections (2004) indicate that in 2004, African American students constituted 16.88% of total school enrollment but only 8.99% of the enrollment in gifted programs. Figures for Hispanics were 18.94% and 12.33%, for English language learners 8.74% and 2.16%, and students with disabilities 12.80% and 2.02%. Examination of data over time suggests that representation of these groups in programs for the gifted has improved little over the last 15 years.

2. *Underachievement.* Analyses of achievement data suggest that African Americans, Latinos, and Native Americans are underrepresented among the highest levels of achievement across socioeconomic groups (College Board, 1999; Miller, 2004).

3. *Bias and discrimination.* Discrimination contributes to the achievement gap (College Board, 1999). From a social reconstructionist perspective, teachers and administrators can work to ameliorate historic and continuing discrimination experienced by individuals of color. Gifted students—who will be leaders in their chosen fields—have potential to contribute to positive social change.

4. *Benefits of multicultural education for all.* Teachers' use of challenging, multicultural curriculum supports the academic achievement of all students, including students from low-income and culturally and linguistically diverse backgrounds (VanTassel-Baska & Stambaugh, 2006b). Additionally, multicultural curriculum enhances openness to racial understanding and prepares students for success in a multicultural society (Kurlaender & Yun, 2001).

5. *Need for sensitive teachers.* Some teachers, however unintentionally, fail to recognize the talents of students from culturally and linguistically diverse backgrounds (e.g., Elhoweris, Mutua, Alsheikh, & Holloway, 2005; Peterson & Margolin, 1997). More bilingual teachers (Bernal, 2002) and teachers of color (Ford & Trotman, 2001) are needed in gifted education. However, being bilingual or of color does not in itself ensure teacher sensitivity or student achievement (García & Guerra, 2004). Moreover, teachers from all backgrounds can work effectively with gifted students of color (Ford & Trotman, 2001; Harmon, 2002).

CONTENT AND STRATEGIES FOR IMPLEMENTING DIVERSITY STANDARDS

A major challenge for professional development in the area of diversity concerns the scarcity of research linking specific professional development approaches to teacher

Table 9.1　Knowledge and Skill Standards Specifically Addressing Diversity

Standard	Description
Standard 1: Foundations	Educators of the gifted understand the historical foundations of the field, including points of view and contributions of individuals from diverse backgrounds. They consider the impact of the dominant culture's role in shaping schools and potential differences between school and home cultures. They further comprehend how issues of diversity affect families, cultures, and schools as well as the delivery of gifted educational services.
Standard 2: Development and Characteristics of Learners	Educators of the gifted understand the cognitive and affective characteristics of individuals with gifts and talents from diverse backgrounds and effects of culture on development.
Standard 3: Individual Learning Differences	Educators of the gifted consider how language, culture, and family background affect academic and social behavior, learning patterns, attitudes, values, and interests. They understand the influence of different beliefs and values across and within groups on relationships involving the gifted, their families, schools, and communities. They integrate perspectives of diverse groups into instructional planning.
Standard 4: Instructional Strategies	Educators of the gifted use evidence-based curriculum and instructional strategies to promote challenging learning opportunities and enhance self-awareness and self-efficacy. They engage gifted and talented learners from all backgrounds in challenging multicultural curricula. Educators of the gifted use assistive technologies to meet the needs of gifted students with disabilities.
Standard 5: Learning Environments and Social Interactions	Educators of the gifted create learning environments that foster cultural understanding and appreciation, environments in which diversity is valued and individuals learn to live harmoniously and productively. Educators of the gifted understand ways in which groups are stereotyped and experience historical and current discrimination and implications for education. They support development of social interaction and coping skills to address personal and social issues, including discrimination and stereotyping.
Standard 6: Language and Communication	Educators of the gifted understand the influence of diversity on communication and match their communication to students' language proficiency and cultural and linguistic differences. They facilitate acquisition of subject matter for gifted English language learners and use assistive technologies to enhance communication of gifted learners with disabilities.
Standard 7: Instructional Planning	Within the context of long-range plans, educators of the gifted consider an individual's abilities and needs, the learning environment, and cultural and linguistic factors in setting objectives, selecting/adapting/creating materials, and using differentiated instructional strategies.
Standard 8: Assessment	Educators of the gifted understand the process and principles of identification, measurement, and placement for individuals with gifts and talents from culturally and linguistically diverse backgrounds. They use nonbiased and equitable approaches for identifying diverse gifted learners, including alternative assessments.
Standard 9: Professional and Ethical Practice	Educators of the gifted recognize that culture and language interact with gifts and talents and are sensitive to the many aspects of diversity among gifted learners and their families. They reflect on their own personal and cultural frames of reference that affect their teaching, including biases about individuals from diverse backgrounds. Educators of the gifted encourage and model respect for the full range of diversity among gifted individuals.
Standard 10: Collaboration	Educators of the gifted understand culturally responsive behaviors that promote effective communication and collaboration with gifted individuals, their families, school personnel, and community members. They collaborate and consult with school personnel about the characteristics and needs of gifted individuals from diverse backgrounds and those with disabilities.

and student outcomes. However, the few studies that address student outcomes suggest professional development can make a difference for diverse students (Knight & Wiseman, 2005).

Space limitations do not permit comprehensive discussion of content and strategies for all diversity standards and all forms of diversity. Based on what we know about effective teachers of diverse gifted students, this section provides guidance on selected professional development goals for (a) teachers' cultural awareness and self-reflection, (b) supporting gifted learners from racially diverse backgrounds, and (c) using multicultural curriculum to enhance the learning of all students.

Effective Teachers of Diverse Students

Though based on small numbers, Harmon's (2002) study of teachers identified as effective and ineffective by gifted African American students offers insights for professional development. Ineffective teachers communicated low expectations of African American students and behaved in ways that appeared disrespectful and prejudicial. They lacked understanding of these students' needs and did not intervene to eliminate name-calling and harassment. In contrast, effective teachers held high expectations and were respectful of all students, understood students' culture, implemented multicultural curriculum, explained concepts in accessible ways, used cooperative learning, discussed coping skills for dealing with racism, provided a disciplined classroom, and did not tolerate name-calling and harassment.

Harmon's findings are consistent with Ford and Trotman's (2001) identified multicultural competencies for teachers of the gifted: self- and cultural awareness; social responsibility manifested in increasing multicultural understanding among and providing multicultural education to all students, even in homogenous settings; and using culturally sensitive instructional practices.

Cultural Awareness and Understanding

It is important to note that institutions provide the policies and contexts in which teachers practice and that systemic factors, such as required use of biased identification criteria and instruments, contribute to continued inequities in identification and services. Most teachers have positive intentions yet may be unaware of "deficit" thinking that inhibits high expectations and culturally consonant practice (García & Guerra, 2004). Assuming that poverty, race, or primary language inhibits learning and failing to consider external factors that produce risk (school-, classroom-, teacher-, pedagogy-related variables) are examples of deficit thinking (García & Guerra, 2004). According to García and Guerra, teachers who express deep concern for students often put caring and stability ahead of academics, underestimating students' ability to learn.

To encourage awareness and examination of assumptions (Standard 9), García and Guerra (2004) recommend professional development activities that produce cognitive dissonance, including problem-based activities requiring teachers to analyze a specific situation, develop hypotheses about contributing factors, consider alternative cultural explanations (which requires cultural knowledge), and identify culturally responsive strategies to resolve the situation. Ford (Milner & Ford, 2005) describes a simulation consistent with this model that enables teachers to begin the long-term process of self-reflection. As the instructor, she provides profiles of ten students, including two students of color: one high achieving with a high intelligence test score and one with high grades, an average intelligence test score, and a history of leadership and service activities. The task is for teachers, in small groups, to reach consensus on six students they will recommend for placement in gifted education. Teachers present their recommendations and rationale, and the whole group examines the profiles of those recommended and not recommended, including gender, types of giftedness, and race. The activity enables Ford to introduce the question of whether race matters in delivering services to gifted and talented students (Standard 1).

The types of inservice strategies most likely to promote teachers' cultural competence are not clear, though workshops with teacher interaction and reflection followed up by coaching and consulting appear to support positive outcomes (Knight & Wiseman, 2005). When teachers report increased cultural sensitivity and awareness through professional development, the change does not necessarily result in culturally responsive practice or higher levels of student performance (García & Guerra, 2004). To increase effectiveness, inservice training needs to demonstrate a clear link to student outcomes.

Cultural Knowledge and Culturally Consonant Instruction

Knowledge of the values, beliefs, and culturally related behaviors of families served is critical for teachers' understanding of students' learning needs and behaviors (Standard 3). A number of sources provide culture-specific information on children and families in general (Lynch & Hanson, 2004; Shade, Kelly, & Oberg, 1997) and characteristics specific to gifted students from diverse backgrounds (e.g., Castellano, 2003). Culture-specific knowledge can support teachers' efforts to understand student behavior. For example, a teacher described a Filipino student identified as gifted as a slow reader and was considering referral for a learning disability. In reading about Filipino culture (Litton, 1999), the teacher found that some students read slowly and carefully, memorizing parts. This explanation fit with the observed behavior of the student, which the teacher confirmed through discussion with the student.

Some experts (e.g., Cazden & Mehan, 1989) argue that professional development should have the goal of enabling teachers to use observation and interview to gain understanding of individual students and families, as learning about specific cultures may lead to overgeneralization, inaccurate assumptions, and stereotyping. A practical middle ground between acquiring culture-specific information and learning how to understand specific students and families is to develop background knowledge of specific cultures and look for individual differences within a cultural group. For example, understanding ethnic identity development among African American gifted students can help teachers support students' social/emotional growth (Ford, Moore, & Milner, 2005). At the same time, there are individual differences among African Americans regarding the salience of African American identity (Rowley & Moore, 2002).

Professional development on culture-specific knowledge related to values, beliefs, and concerns about schooling can also support teachers' communication with parents and families (Standard 10). Ford (2004a) and Huff, Houskamp, Watkins, Stanton, and Tavegia (2005) describe the particular concerns of African American parents of gifted students, which few programs address. Morissette (2006) found that parents of low-income gifted students, like other parents of the gifted, desire information about the characteristics and behaviors of gifted students and how to manage them. In addition, they expressed a need for "hands-on" activities to understand how to assist their children with schoolwork as well as simultaneous translation during parent meetings.

Understanding culture-specific values, beliefs, and approaches to teaching and learning can support teachers' efforts to provide instruction consonant with students' preferred approaches to learning. Research conducted with Native Hawaiian, Native American, and other cultural groups suggests that enabling students to connect their cultural resources to new academic content, for example through culturally familiar forms of participation, facilitates their learning (Wills, Lintz, & Mehan, 2004).

Culturally consonant instruction for gifted English language learners focuses on programs and strategies consistent with their language characteristics (Standard 6) (Castellano & Diaz, 2002; Kitano & Pedersen, 2002b) as well as learning goals. For example, dual-language programs support development and maintenance of both English and the student's first language.

Videotaped interactions between teachers and students serve as a stimulus for applying García and Guerra's (2004) professional development approach, in this case to the application of culture-specific knowledge. For example, this author shows teachers a videotaped observation of a highly gifted African American boy in an elementary classroom. The first scene captures the student fiddling with string as the teacher delivers a science lecture to the whole group. The teacher interrupts herself to take the string away and ask the student to move to the back of the classroom. The teacher next asks two White male students to help her demonstrate the first part of a science experiment that all students will replicate and then complete through independent inquiry. She assigns students to work in pairs. The gifted student leaves his partner (a White girl) to seek assistance from the two boys who helped the teacher and then from the teacher herself. All ignore him. When students reconvene as a group to share observations and draw generalizations, the African American gifted student offers an off-color rhyme and again is asked to leave the group.

When teachers are invited to analyze the situation, a typical initial response is to describe the videotaped teacher's efforts as reactively ignoring problem behavior to extinguish it. As they gather cultural information about family interaction patterns and student needs and approaches to learning, they hypothesize that the student's negative behavior may be reactive when his needs for direct instruction, warmth, and affirmation are rebuffed. Working together, teachers apply their growing cultural knowledge to suggest positive strategies for encouraging the gifted student's learning.

Challenging Multicultural Curriculum

A growing literature suggests that providing a challenging multicultural curriculum (Standard 4) benefits all learners, including White students. Systematic professional development with explicit links to classroom practice can enable teachers to implement a multicultural curriculum, resulting in increased student achievement and critical thinking (VanTassel-Baska & Stambaugh, 2006b). Using the William and Mary language arts units designed for high-ability students, VanTassel-Baska and Stambaugh's professional development approach included introducing the model for teaching, modeling a lesson, providing practice using the model with feedback, and debriefing the lesson. Results indicated effective teacher use of strategies and significant achievement gains among all ability, economic, and ethnic groups.

Multicultural curriculum, like any curriculum for gifted learners, requires consistency with content standards, a coherent theoretical framework, and rigor in expected conceptual and thinking process outcomes. Professional development can support teachers' implementation of challenging multicultural curriculum through (a) research-supported curriculum units developed specifically for advanced learners (e.g., William and Mary; STAR) or (b) models for developing multicultural curriculum units (e.g., Ford & Harris, 1999; Pedersen & Kitano, 2006).

The William and Mary Language Arts, Social Studies, and Science curricula were designed for high-ability students based on VanTassel-Baska's (2003a) Integrated Curriculum Model. The model integrates advanced content in the discipline, higher-order thinking through specific reasoning and research models, and learning experiences around concepts, issues, and themes (e.g., change, cause and effect, systems). Evaluation studies using large samples support the curriculum's effectiveness for gifted students across diverse income and ethnic groups.

The Ford and Harris (1999) model integrates, through a two-dimensional matrix, Banks's four levels of multicultural goals and Bloom's taxonomy of educational objectives. The model can be applied across a range of subject matter areas and enables teachers to encourage students to examine multicultural content through a contributions, additive, transformative, or social action lens using specific thinking processes (knowledge, comprehension, application, analysis, synthesis, and evaluation). For example, a social action/evaluation activity might involve students in examining school policies to determine whether they support democratic ideals (Ford & Harris, 1999). Teachers find the model accessible and useful in developing and revising lessons and units.

Pedersen and Kitano's (2006) framework employs a cognitive-developmental approach to children's understanding of (a) racial concepts and (b) coping strategies for dealing with stressful encounters over the life span (Standard 5). Teachers assess students' conceptual level with respect to diversity and coping strategies, identify objectives, and integrate them with curriculum standards. For example, applied to multicultural literature, students infer the author's thinking about ethnic pride, consider how the setting depicts the social issues of the time, and evaluate the effectiveness of a character's coping strategies in response to the central conflict. While in a preliminary stage of development, this model enables teachers to identify developmentally appropriate social and cognitive learning objectives.

Professional development can encourage teachers to integrate their assumptions concerning expectations for diverse learners, their growing cultural knowledge, and increased skill in developing challenging curriculum. A sample exercise supporting this goal engages teachers in analyzing pairs of instructional activities in terms of their appropriateness for gifted students of color. Haycock's (2006) examples of lessons provided by two different teachers at the same grade level illustrate teachers' power to influence student achievement through level of expectation and rigor. Comparison of the lessons' standards, objectives, methods, and materials encourage teachers to ponder their own expectations. Having teachers revise the first activity to increase cultural relevance and the second activity to increase rigor encourages understanding that the curriculum can simultaneously address high standards and diversity content. These activities also encourage discussion of what constitutes culturally consonant instruction for gifted students.

A frequent theme in literature is the conflict between the individual and society. From literature you have read, select a character who struggled with society. In a well-developed essay, identify the character and explain why this character's conflict with society is important.

Write a composition of at least 4 paragraphs on Martin Luther King's most important contribution to this society. Illustrate your work with a neat cover page. Neatness counts. (Haycock, 2006, Slides 128–129)

Implementation Issues

Elementary and secondary teachers of the gifted who implement multicultural goals report a number of benefits, including more accepting behavior, increased knowledge of social issues, greater appreciation for diverse cultures and perspectives, lively discussions, and increased self-esteem and motivation (Kitano & Pedersen, 2002a). They also identify reasons for hesitancy, such as concerns about relevance to standards, lack of training and materials, anticipated family and student responses, and lack of confidence in managing discussions about race, culture, disability, sexual orientation, and prejudice. Working with mentors, keeping parents informed, consulting with colleagues, and gaining experience in using the language of difference can allay apprehensions.

Effective professional development on diversity standards is likely to be incremental and long-term (Schniedewind, 2005), particularly where goals include fostering critical multicultural education and working toward social change in schools. Given limited research linking professional development in diversity to teacher and student outcomes (Knight & Wiseman, 2005), school districts could contribute critical information by assessing the impact of specific professional development activities on teacher practice and student performance. The literature documents persistent underidentification and underachievement of gifted students in some ethnic, language, economic, and disability groups and the positive impact of challenging multicultural curriculum for all learners. For these reasons, professional development and assessment on the diversity standards demand attention.

10

Challenges
and Prospects

Susan K. Johnsen, Joyce VanTassel-Baska,
Diane Montgomery, and Margie Kitano

Agreement by the major national professional organizations on what entry-level teachers of the gifted should know and be able to do constitutes a major step forward in designing preservice and inservice programs that will improve services to gifted and talented learners. The national standards, with their emphasis on many forms of diversity, offer promise for better meeting the needs of underserved gifted students, including those from culturally and linguistically diverse backgrounds, those with economic disadvantage, and those with disabilities. Yet the standards themselves will have no impact unless PreK–12 schools commit to their use as guides for identifying, supporting, and assessing teachers of the gifted. What are the challenges that must be overcome to ensure widespread use of the standards? What opportunities and prospects for the future can support our efforts?

CHALLENGES AND ISSUES

Challenges include the need for voluntary commitment to standards-based professional development in the absence of state and federal mandates, assessment of effectiveness of typical workshops on changing practice and student learning, and coordinating professional development among categorical and subject matter programs to support teachers' efforts to integrate often disparately presented professional development activities.

Committing to Standards-Based Professional Development

Only 18 states mandate the preparation of teachers in gifted education. Of those that do mandate, requirements range from 30 clock hours of professional development to 18 or more graduate hours that lead to a master's degree. When policy does not require the preparation of teachers in gifted education, schools must assume this important role through professional development activities or partnerships with universities or other service agencies. When implementing any change or reform such as the development of teachers' knowledge and skills in serving gifted students, the most successful approaches are those that involve both "grassroots" and administrative commitments.

At the administrative level, a rationale for needing professional development that is aligned with the new standards might be supported by identifying (a) the value added by current programs that are effective in serving gifted and talented students as measured by state or national achievement tests, (b) the value added by general education programs that use differentiation strategies for all students, (c) the achievement gaps among different groups of gifted students in their talent areas such as those from lower-income or minority groups, and (d) needs expressed by the school board, principals, and community members (see Table 5.1 for identifying specific professional development objectives).

At the grassroots, or parent and teacher, level, the rationale might be based on identifying (a) the quality of work in classrooms that are effective in serving gifted and talented students as assessed by classroom products and performances, (b) the quality of work of all students in classrooms that use differentiated instructional practices, (c) case study or action research that shows the improvements in students' engagement, products, or performances when they are in classrooms with teachers who have been prepared to teach gifted students, and (d) needs expressed by teachers, parents, and other community members (see Table 7.1 for other ways of collecting information through professional development activities). When administrators, teachers, parents, and other community members' assessments merge into a common vision for gifted education, standards-based development of teachers is more likely to occur and be successful in spite of weak or no mandates.

Assessing Effects of Professional Development on Teacher Practice and Student Learning

Educators know the benefits of and necessity for evaluating educational activities and instructional strategies. Yet planning for the evaluation of professional development is challenging. Often, the outcome for evaluation is unclear or rests solely with the consumer—the teacher participating in the professional development activity. In the absence of a clear statement of expected outcomes, assessment becomes artificial and temporal, focusing instead on organization of presentation, degree to which immediate application is possible, temperature of the room, or the quality of the food. The 10 standards, each with several knowledge and skills, can help professional development planners identify specific expected outcomes for short- and long-term training activities.

A number of strategies are becoming available to assist teachers and supervisors assess the extent to which professional development activities supported changes in instructional practice and student outcomes (see Chapter 8). Teachers can engage in self-evaluation or request peer feedback from fellow teachers, site administrators, or mentors. Self-evaluation might include setting a clear outcome expectation for students related to the training content and standards (e.g., Standard 4, students will analyze critical social issues through challenging multicultural curriculum). They would compare the depth and detail of student knowledge on a social issue using pre/postessays. Professional development coordinators can team with teachers in using pre-/post-concept mapping to determine teacher growth in concept acquisition. Peer coaches can observe changes in teacher instructional behaviors and student engagement using instruments such as those in Appendix A. Whatever assessment strategy is used, it should be made clear to teachers at the outset that what is being evaluated is the quality of professional development activities rather than the particular teacher.

Coordinating Professional Development Among Categorical and Subject Matter Programs

One strategy for ensuring that a standards-based approach to professional development occurs in gifted education is to establish collaborative relationships with relevant departments in the central office. Aspects of implementation of the standards lend themselves to joint inservice training to focus on the following topics:

- Diversity
- Twice exceptional learners
- Content area curriculum adaptations of curriculum PreK–12
- Counseling and guidance of the gifted

Cost- and resource-sharing approaches need to be employed to ensure that these topics are adequately addressed in relevant contexts with teachers and administrative staffs. For these professional development efforts to work effectively, the gifted program coordinator must orchestrate a three-year professional development plan that targets areas of the standards each year for relevant groups. Year 1, for example, could feature a diversity and differentiation in content areas goal, Year 2 a counseling and guidance goal, and Year 3, an instructional differentiation goal. Each goal needs to be translated into a model such as seen in Table 10.1. A cost analysis also should be performed to ensure that collaborators also contribute appropriately.

Table 10.1   Sample District Professional Development Plan

Goal	Collaborations	Target Audience	Outcomes	Assessment
To enhance understanding of diversity issues in classrooms and schools	Special education, minority achievement, gifted, and English language learner programs	All classroom teachers and principals	• Use of differential approaches, based on intellectual, cultural, and social differences • Incorporation of positive role models, representative of diverse groups • Incorporation of diverse materials	Principal monitoring of classrooms
To develop adaptive curricula for use with diverse learners	Content specialists in reading, language arts, math, science, and social studies	Relevant teachers, G/T specialists	Adapted curriculum based on content standards	Content expert and G/T coordinator monitoring of classrooms

OPPORTUNITIES

Opportunities include linking with university partners, incorporating promising teaching and learning technologies, and providing leadership in improving outcomes for gifted and talented learners.

Linking With University Partners

Universities may be a resource for school districts that are planning and implementing standards-based professional development. Levels of involvement may include (a) assessing school district needs, (b) leading professional development workshops and follow-through activities, (c) providing one or more university- or school-based courses, (d) evaluating the effectiveness of programs, (e) establishing professional development schools that emphasize gifted education, or (f) conducting action research. In assessing school district needs, university and school faculty can review the alignment between school, state, and national standards; observe classrooms and programs; survey stakeholders; and identify possible areas that may need to be addressed through professional development activities. These professional development activities would then be led by school or university faculty, depending on different individuals' expertise.

Some school districts may want to require a master's level certificate for teachers with primary responsibility for working with gifted and talented students or at least one course for general education teachers. Course content might not only be aligned with standards but be collaboratively determined by the school district and the university based on the school's needs assessment. Course options might also be a part of a teacher's individual development plan (see Chapter 4). School districts might want university faculty to evaluate their programs formally to provide a stronger rationale for standards-based professional development. At a more involved level, schools and universities might decide to establish professional development schools where continual action research defines best practices and ultimately professional development needs. In all these university partnerships, collaboration and mutual respect are keys to the attainment of common goals.

Incorporating Promising Technologies

School districts are increasingly taking advantage of computer and Internet technologies to support standards-based professional development. Examples include e-portfolios, learning management systems, and video-based learning tools. TaskStream (www.taskstream.com) is one example of a commercial e-portfolio being used by university teacher preparation programs and school districts engaged in providing standards-based induction and other professional development. Instructors use TaskStream to develop, document, and share standards-based learning activities and resources and to build and apply assessment rubrics linked to standards. TaskStream enables teachers to build personal e-portfolios linked to specific standards, which are shared with instructors for receiving feedback. The system enables instructors to determine who has met specific standards at specific competence levels, by individual or in aggregate.

Learning management systems help educators to create online workshops and courses with opportunities for building learning communities. Moodle (www.moodle.org), for example, is an open source learning management system that enables professional development staff to build e-learning experiences with tools for organizing content, hosting forums and chats, sharing event calendars, and giving assignments. Teachers can upload lesson plans for evaluation and sharing.

A number of public (e.g., county office of education) and commercial organizations are building and offering computer-based "assets" in the form of learning modules or entire courses and programs for standards-based professional development. One format with high potential for use in professional development includes video clips of teachers using research-based instructional strategies (e.g., methods for English language learners). Modules may include such features as (a) simultaneous scrolling text directing the viewer to salient features of the video, (b) summaries of the method's theoretical underpinnings and defining elements, (c) video of expert commentary on the method, (d) learning activities to support teacher implementation, and (e) links to standards.

Providing Leadership in Moving the Field Forward

A multitude of research studies identify teachers as the most critical factor in improving student learning, including that of students from culturally and linguistically diverse backgrounds. PreK–12 school personnel can raise the quality of schooling for gifted and talented students by implementing standards-based practices in identification, assessment, curriculum and instruction, and collaboration with colleagues and families. Adopting the national standards in assigning and developing teachers of the gifted is one powerful way of ensuring positive change. Given the numbers of identified and unidentified gifted students enrolled in general education classrooms, districts can incorporate appropriate standards into professional development of general education teachers as well. Sharing with other districts professional development strategies that result in improved teaching and learning will move the field forward in serving gifted students and their families.

Appendix A

Observation Instruments

Differentiated Classroom Observation on Scale Protocol

Preobservation Phase

Before going to the teacher, the observer will contact the teacher to find a time that is convenient for the observation.

The following will need to be arranged before the observation date:

- Permission to observe from teacher
- Copy of lesson plan
- Teacher will visually identify targeted group of students in classroom (with color-coded name tags or teacher's chosen strategy)
- Teacher is made aware that there is a brief (5 minutes or so) preobservation interview, and a short postobservation debriefing.

Preobservation Interview

Before beginning the interview, please arrange to have the following questions answered. Some of this will be facilitated with prior contact with the teacher. In particular, having a copy of the lesson plan in advance would make the following questions less laborious for the teacher to answer prior to the observation period. This is an informal interview that is merely to gain essential descriptive information.

1. Is this lesson tiered?
   - __ Yes (based on identification status)
   - __ Yes (not based on identification status)
   - __ Not explicitly, but cluster grouping will be used
   - __ No, all students completing same activities

2. Who developed this lesson?
   - __ This teacher
   - __ Other: _____

3. How closely will you be following the predesigned lesson plan?

4. Have you used this lesson before?
   What success have you noted with this lesson regarding this identified population?

5. Are learning contracts being used?
   - __ Yes (multiple-identified students)
   - __ Yes (single-identified student)
   - __ Yes (not related to identified status)
   - __ Yes (IEP-determined)
   - __ No

6. Has any of this lesson been compacted for any child?
   If so, please explain the alternate learning activities that are substituting for the lesson.

7. What are the goals/objectives of this lesson?

8. Anything else the teacher wants to add before the observation:

Classroom Observation Phase

School: _____ Teacher: _____

Time of observation: _____

Total number of students: _____ Number from identified group: _____

List additional adults in room, including time in room, role, and number of children served:

Five-Minute Segment Scoring (use DCOS Scoring Sheet)

During the observation period, please indicate for each five-minute segment which of the following instructional activities were in practice. There will be at least one per segment, and each segment will likely have more than one. The segment ratings should be marked separately for the two groups of students: "identified" and "not identified." In the event that there is no way to distinguish between the two groups, make whole-group ratings in the "not identified" group location only.

In addition to the instructional activities, please also rate student engagement, cognitive level, and "learning director" for each five-minute segment.

Instructional Activity Codes		
Instructional Activity	**Code**	**Description**
Lecture	L	Teacher lecturing to group of students
Lecture with discussion	LD	Teacher-led lecture, with periodic discussion (recitation)
Class discussion	CD	Discussion in class, students are primary discussants
Small-group discussion	GD	Discussion in class, but in small groups, not whole group
Problem modeling by teacher	PM	Teacher demonstrating how to execute a task (e.g., working a math problem on board)
Student presentation	SP	Student(s) presenting information to the class (either planned presentation or on-demand task)
Demonstration by teacher	D	Teacher demonstrating a procedure to the class (e.g., how to safely use lab equipment)
Questioning by teacher	Q	Teacher asking questions of students in group setting
Student responding	SR	Student(s) answering questions posed by teacher (choral response included in this category)
Manipulatives	M	Student(s) working with concrete materials to illustrate abstract concepts (e.g., math blocks)
Cubing	C	Student(s) working with cubing curriculum materials (differentiated, see Adams & Pierce, 2006*, for details)

*Adams, C. M., & Pierce, R. L. (2003). *Teaching by tiering. Science & Children, 41*(3), 30–34.

Instructional Activity Codes		
Instructional Activity	**Code**	**Description**
Learning centers	LC	Student(s) working at planned learning centers individually or in small groups (computer stations can be included if they are planned activities)
Anchoring activity before lesson	AB	Use of lesson-anchoring materials prior to teacher presentation of content (see Adams & Pierce, 2006*, for details)
Anchoring activity during lesson	AD	Use of lesson-anchoring materials during teacher presentation of content
Anchoring activity after lesson	AA	Use of lesson-anchoring materials after teacher presentation of content
Seat work—individual	SWI	Student(s) working at desk on academic materials (independently)
Seat work—group based	SWG	Student(s) working at desk on academic materials (group)
Cooperative learning	CL	Students working in a planned cooperative structure to complete a task
Role playing	RP	Student(s) engaged in role play exercises (e.g., "playing store" to practice counting change)
Teacher interacting with individual student	TIS	Teacher working with/talking to/helping individual student
Teacher interacting with small group	TIG	Teacher working with/talking to/helping small group of students
Technology use—students	TS	Technology being used by students for related learning activities
Technology use—teacher	TT	Technology being used by the teacher for presenting instructional content
Assessment activity	A	Students engaged in a formalized assessment activity (e.g., test; performance)
Pullout activity—individual or group	PO	Student(s) removed from the room—no observation of these students possible
Other	O	List "other" activities

(Continued)

(Continued)

Student Engagement, Cognitive Activity, and "Learning Director"		
These are global ratings for each five-minute segment. Thus, each segment will have only one rating for each of these two domains, the rating that is most representative of that time period for that group.		
Student Engagement	**Cognitive Activity**	**"Learning Director"**
L—Low engagement = 20% or fewer of students engaged in learning M—Moderate engagement = 21%–79% of students engaged in learning H—High engagement = 80% or more of students engaged in learning	Remember Understand Apply Analyze Evaluate Create Ratings are made in each segment following the given scale: 1—Not evident 2—Evident 3—Well represented	*Who directs the learning, or makes the decisions about the learning activities.* Use the following scale for making your segment ratings for the identified groups: 1—Teacher directs all learning 2—Teacher directs most learning 3—Teacher and student share learning decisions 4—Student directs most learning 5—Student directs all learning

Differentiated Classroom Observation Scale: Scoring Form

			1	2	3	4	5
Identified	**Activity**		L M H	L M H	L M H	L M H	L M H
	Engagement	Remember	1 2 3	1 2 3	1 2 3	1 2 3	1 2 3
		Understand	1 2 3	1 2 3	1 2 3	1 2 3	1 2 3
	Cognitive	Apply	1 2 3	1 2 3	1 2 3	1 2 3	1 2 3
		Analyze	1 2 3	1 2 3	1 2 3	1 2 3	1 2 3
		Evaluate	1 2 3	1 2 3	1 2 3	1 2 3	1 2 3
		Create	1 2 3	1 2 3	1 2 3	1 2 3	1 2 3
	Learning Director		1 2 3 4 5	1 2 3 4 5	1 2 3 4 5	1 2 3 4 5	1 2 3 4 5
Not Identified	**Activity**		1	2	3	4	5
	Engagement		L M H	L M H	L M H	L M H	L M H
		Remember	1 2 3	1 2 3	1 2 3	1 2 3	1 2 3
		Understand	1 2 3	1 2 3	1 2 3	1 2 3	1 2 3
	Cognitive	Apply	1 2 3	1 2 3	1 2 3	1 2 3	1 2 3
		Analyze	1 2 3	1 2 3	1 2 3	1 2 3	1 2 3
		Evaluate	1 2 3	1 2 3	1 2 3	1 2 3	1 2 3
		Create	1 2 3	1 2 3	1 2 3	1 2 3	1 2 3

(Continued)

Holistic Observation Ratings

At the conclusion of the segment ratings, complete the following items, PRIOR TO the teacher debriefing.

Please describe how grouping (if any) occurred in this classroom:
Were differentiated practices used in the classroom for identified and not identified students?
___Yes ___No
If Yes, please rate each of the following items based on your OVERALL perception, for each group separately.
If No, simply respond in the "Not Identified Group" column, using the following scale for both:

SD	D	N	A	SA	NA	
Strongly Disagree	Disagree	Neutral	Agree	Strongly Agree	Not able to respond, lack of evidence (use sparingly)	
					Identified Group	Not Identified Group
This lesson encouraged students to seek and value multiple modes of investigation or problem solving.						
Students were reflective about their learning.						
The instructional strategies and activities respected and accounted for students' prior knowledge.						
Interactions among students demonstrated collaborative learning environment.						
The teacher clearly enjoyed working with this group.						
Teacher demonstrated high level of content knowledge for lesson topic.						
Transitions between activities were smooth and well coordinated.						
Group procedures were clear, established, and understood by the students (automaticity was evident).						
Anchoring activities were readily available and appropriate.						
The classroom management plan was clear and effective.						
Learning activities were primarily student-directed.						
Teacher served primarily as a "Sage on the Stage" to this group.						

Postobservation Debriefing & Reflection

Debriefing With Teacher — Thank the teacher for the observation period, and use this last segment of approximately 5 minutes to clarify anything observed. Then, ask the teacher: *Is there anything you wanted to add regarding the observation before I leave?* (take detailed notes).

Final Reflection — **After leaving the classroom,** take a couple of minutes to make any other written comments that are relevant or make the observation more contextually based or comprehensive. Such issues may include the tone, demeanor, or attitude of the teacher and/or students.

Source: Reprinted with permission from Cassady, J.,et al. (2004).

Classroom Instructional Practices Scale (CIPS)

Research Assistant _____

Teacher _____ Grade _____

School _____ Date/Time Observed _____

Discipline/Subject _____

Content

—— C1 book or curriculum guide organizes content

—— C2 includes creative and critical thinking skills

—— C3 integration of multiple disciplines; single discipline-based topic; not authentic methods

—— C4 interdisciplinary, broad-based themes; authentic methods

—— C5 special attributes of generalization, concepts

—— C6 student performance determines sequence

—— C7 student interest guides content

Rate

—— R1 have same/varied amount of time for tasks; early finishers do no task

—— R2 have same/varied amount of time for tasks; early finishers do an unrelated task

—— R3 have same/varied time for completion of task; early finishers do a related task

Rate With Assessment

—— R4 postassessment at set times with no recycling

—— R5 postassessment at varied times with no recycling

—— R6 postassessment at set times with recycling and/or in-depth study/enrichment/acceleration

—— R7 postassessment at varied times with recycling and/or in-depth study/enrichment/acceleration

—— R8 pre/postassessment at set times with recycling and/or in-depth study/enrichment/acceleration

—— R9 pre/postassessment at varied times with recycling and/or in-depth study/enrichment/acceleration

Environment

—— E1 arrangement with limited student interaction; no interest or learning centers present

—— E2 arrangement with limited student interaction; interest or learning centers present

—— E3 arrangement with student interaction

—— E4 arrangement with limited student interaction; interest centers present

—— E5 arrangement with limited student interaction; learning centers present

—— E6 use of school and/or community as learning centers

Preference

—— P1 no variation in tasks and/or response dimensions; not correlated

—— P2 variation in tasks and/or response dimensions; not correlated

—— P3 no variation in tasks and/or response dimensions; correlated

—— P4 variation in tasks and/or response dimensions; correlated

—— P5 student choice of varied tasks and/or response dimensions

Additional observations in terms of adapting differences:

Source: Reprinted with permission from Johnsen, S. K., et al., (2002).

The William and Mary Classroom Observation Scales Revised

Classroom Observation Scales Development Team:
Joyce VanTassel-Baska, EdD
Linda Avery, PhD
Jeanne Struck, PhD
Annie Feng, EdD
Bruce Bracken, PhD
Diann Drummond, MEd
Tamra Stambaugh, MEd

The College of William and Mary
School of Education
Center for Gifted Education

2003

Funded by the Jacob Javits Grant,
United States Department of Education

The William and Mary Project Athena Observation Scales Guidelines

> ➤ *Please review and follow the protocol outlined below when conducting Project Athena classroom observations.*

> ➤ Introduce yourself and your partner to the classroom teacher.

> ➤ Ask where he or she would like for you to sit during the observation.

> ➤ Confirm your meeting time after the lesson.

> ➤ Complete the demographics section (except the service delivery model) on the Classroom Observation Scale (COS) as available. Confirm the service delivery model with the coordinator.

> ➤ Complete the COS script sheet during the observation.

> ➤ Meet with the teacher to ask the *Teacher Interview Questions*. Write responses on page 14. (Remember, you have less than 15 minutes to meet with the teacher.)

> ➤ Using the results of your script and teacher response data, complete the COS checklist by yourself. Make sure there are no blank items on the COS.

> ➤ Using the results of your script regarding student participation and response, complete the Student Observation Scale (SOS) by yourself.

> ➤ Meet with your partner and reach consensus on the teacher and student observation scales. Together, complete the consensus forms for the teacher observation and student observation. Write the same information in each packet.

> ➤ Together, complete the Treatment Fidelity Form. Write the same information in each packet.

> ➤ Paper clip and submit your packet and your partner's packet for each observation.

> ➤ SMILE AND REPEAT THE PROCEDURE!

> ➤ Note: *It is imperative that all forms be completed on the same day of the observation. However, it is highly improbable that forms can be completed immediately after each observation due to the timing of scheduled observations. Be sure your script is as complete as possible for later reference.*

The William and Mary Classroom Observation Scales, Revised (Part 1)
Teacher Observation

Joyce VanTassel-Baska, EdD Linda Avery, PhD   Jeanne Struck, PhD   Annie Feng, EdD
Bruce Bracken, PhD   Dianne Drummond, MEd Tamra Stambaugh, MEd

---

Observer _____   Date _____ # of minutes observed _____

School _____   Grade _____

Teacher _____   Course/Lesson Observed _____

Student Information: Total # _____

Observed Gender: #Boys _____   #Girls _____

Observed Ethnicity: #White _____   #African American _____ #Hispanic _____

                          #Asian American _____   #Other _____

Gifted: #Identified Gifted _____

Classroom Desk Arrangement: Desks in rows and columns __ Desks in groups __ Desks in circle __

Other (specify) _____

Service Delivery Model: *(as designated by the coordinator)*

            Self-Contained ____ Inclusion ____ Cluster Group ____ Pullout ____ Other_____

Please outline what you have observed in the classroom with respect to curriculum and instruction-related activities. Describe the specific lesson, its organization, instructional methods used, characteristics of the learning experience and environment, texts and materials used, questions asked by the teacher, and any other relevant observations and impressions that may influence your completion of the attached checklist.

Lesson Outline: *(See attached lesson plan script)*

Texts and Materials: *(List any materials, novels, texts, etc., used by students and/or the teacher.)*

Teacher Interview Questions

Discuss the following questions with the teacher observed after each observation period. (Approximate time: 15 minutes)

1. Did you have a written lesson plan for this lesson? ___ yes ___ no

2. How would you characterize the purpose of the lesson?

3. What were your instructional objectives for the previous lesson with this class?

4. What content will you cover in your subsequent lesson?

5. What plans do you have to address homework or extensions of this lesson?

6. How do you intend to assess outcomes for this lesson? Final outcomes for the unit?

7. Are there any aspects of the lesson you would like to clarify before this observation is finalized?

Write responses on the Teacher Interview Form.

The William and Mary Classroom Observation Scales, Revised (Part 2)
Teacher Observation
Joyce VanTassel-Baska, EdD *Linda Avery, PhD*   *Jeanne Struck, PhD*   *Annie Feng, EdD*
Bruce Bracken, PhD   *Dianne Drummond, MEd* *Tamra Stambaugh, MEd*

Directions: Please employ the following scale as you rate each of the checklist items. Rate each item according to how well the teacher characteristic or behavior was demonstrated during the observed instructional activity. Each item is judged on an individual, self-contained basis, regardless of its relationship to an overall set of behaviors relevant to the cluster heading.

3 = Effective	2 = Somewhat Effective	1 = Ineffective	N/O = Not Observed
The teacher evidenced careful planning and classroom flexibility in implementation of the behavior, eliciting many appropriate student responses. The teacher was clear and sustained focus on the purposes of learning.	The teacher evidenced some planning and/or classroom flexibility in implementation of the behavior, eliciting some appropriate student responses. The teacher was sometimes clear and focused on the purposes of learning.	The teacher evidenced little or no planning and/or classroom flexibility in implementation of the behavior, eliciting minimal appropriate student responses. The teacher was unclear and unfocused regarding the purpose of learning.	The listed behavior was not demonstrated during the time of the observation. (NOTE: There must be an obvious attempt made for the certain behavior to be rated "ineffective" instead of "not observed.")

General Teaching Behaviors

Curriculum Planning and Delivery	3	2	1	N/O
The teacher . . .				
1. set high expectations for student performance.				
2. incorporated activities for students to apply new knowledge.				
3. engaged students in planning, monitoring, or assessing their learning.				
4. encouraged students to express their thoughts.				
5. had students reflect on what they had learned.				
Comments:				

(Continued)

(Continued)

Differentiated Teaching Behaviors				
Accommodations for Individual Differences	*3*	*2*	*1*	*N/O*
The teacher . . .				
6. provided opportunities for independent or group learning to promote depth in understanding content.				
7. accommodated individual or subgroup differences (e.g., through individual conferencing, student or teacher choice in material selection, and task assignments.)				
8. encouraged multiple interpretations of events and situations.				
9. allowed students to discover key ideas individually through structured activities and/or questions.				
Comments:				
Problem Solving	*3*	*2*	*1*	*N/O*
The teacher . . .				
10. employed brainstorming techniques.				
11. engaged students in problem identification and definition.				
12. engaged students in solution-finding activities and comprehensive solution articulation.				
Comments:				
Critical Thinking Strategies	*3*	*2*	*1*	*N/O*
The teacher . . .				
13. encouraged students to judge or evaluate situations, problems, or issues.				
14. engaged students in comparing and contrasting ideas (e.g., analyze generated ideas).				
15. provided opportunities for students to generalize from concrete data or information to the abstract.				
16. encouraged student synthesis or summary of information within or across disciplines.				
Comments:				

Creative Thinking Strategies	3	2	1	N/O
The teacher . . .				
17. solicited many diverse thoughts about issues or ideas.				
18. engaged students in the exploration of diverse points of view to reframe ideas.				
19. encouraged students to demonstrate open-mindedness and tolerance of imaginative, sometimes playful solutions to problems.				
20. provided opportunities for students to develop and elaborate on their ideas.				
Comments:				

Research Strategies	3	2	1	N/O
(It is atypical for these to be observed in one session. Some teachers, however, may use Items 21–25 within a single period to illustrate the full research process to students. Please note those observations in the comments section.)				
The teacher . . .				
21. required students to gather evidence from multiple sources through research-based techniques (e.g., print, nonprint, Internet, self-investigation via surveys, interviews, etc.).				
22. provided opportunities for students to analyze data and represent it in appropriate charts, graphs, or tables.				
23. asked questions to assist students in making inferences from data and drawing conclusions.				
24. encouraged students to determine implications and consequences of findings.				
25. provided time for students to communicate research study findings to relevant audiences in a formal report and/or presentation.				
Comments:				

Additional Comments:

The William and Mary Classroom Observation Scales, Revised (Part 3) *Student Observation*

Joyce VanTassel-Baska, EdD   Bruce Bracken, PhD   Dianne Drummond, MEd

---

Student Responses to General Classroom Teacher Behaviors

Engaged in General Classroom Behaviors Students:	*Most* >75%	*Many* 50%–75%	*Some* 25%–50%	*Few* <25%	*None*	*N/A*
1. demonstrated a high level of performance.						
2. applied new learning.						
3. demonstrated planful, monitoring, or evaluating behavior.						
4. articulated thinking process (e.g., verbal mediation).						
5. reflected on learning.						

Comments:

Student Responses to Differentiated Teaching Behaviors

Engaged in Diverse Self-Selected or Self-Paced Activities Students:	*Most* >75%	*Many* 50%–75%	*Some* 25%–50%	*Few* <25%	*None*	*N/A*
6. worked on projects individually or in pairs/groups.						
7. worked on tiered assignments or tasks of choice.						
8. explored multiple interpretations.						
9. discovered central ideas through structured activities and/or questions asked.						

Comments:

Engaged in Problem-Solving Strategies Students:	*Most* >75%	*Many* 50%–75%	*Some* 25%–50%	*Few* <25%	*None*	*N/A*
10. brainstormed ideas or alternative possibilities.						
11. defined problems.						
12. identified and implemented solutions to problems.						

Comments:

Engaged in Critical Thinking Strategies *Students:*	*Most* *>75%*	*Many* *50%–75%*	*Some* *25%–50%*	*Few* *<25%*	*None*	*N/A*
13. made judgments about or evaluated situations, problems, or issues.						
14. compared and contrasted ideas and concepts.						
15. generalized from specific to abstract data or information.						
16. synthesized or summarized information within or across disciplines.						

Comments:

Engaged in Creative Thinking Strategies *Students:*	*Most* *>75%*	*Many* *50%–75%*	*Some* *25%–50%*	*Few* *<25%*	*None*	*N/A*
17. demonstrated ideational fluency.						
18. explored diverse ways to think about a situation/object/event.						
19. offered imaginative, sometimes playful, suggestions as solutions to problems.						
20. provided examples and illustrations of ideas.						

Comments:

Engaged in Research Strategies *Students:*	*Most* *>75%*	*Many* *50%–75%*	*Some* *25%–50%*	*Few* *<25%*	*None*	*N/A*
21. gathered evidence through research techniques (e.g., surveys, interviews, analysis of primary and secondary source documents).						
22. manipulated and transformed data to be interpreted.						
23. made inferences from data and drew conclusions.						
24. determined the implications and consequences of situations.						
25. communicated findings (e.g., report, oral presentation).						

Comments:

Consensus Form

The William and Mary Classroom Observation Scales, Revised (Part 4)
Treatment Fidelity

Directions: The following observation scale addresses the fidelity of implementation in the William and Mary Language Arts units. After reaching consensus with your observation partner, please check the relevant category describing the teacher's implementation of key instructional models.

Lesson # ____					
The teacher . . .	*Effective*	*Somewhat Effective*	*Ineffective*	*N/A*	*Comments*
Content					
1. instructed/practiced literary analysis and interpretation (literature web).					
2. instructed/practiced word analysis (vocabulary web).					
3. instructed/practiced persuasive writing (hamburger model).					
4. instructed/practiced grammar activities.					
5. structured questions for discussion of readings.					
6. enhanced oral communication.					
Process					
7. instructed/practiced the reasoning model.					
8. instructed/practiced the research model.					
Concept					
9. instructed/practiced concept mapping.					
10. emphasized "change" in instruction and assignments.					
11. instructed/applied unit generalizations about change.					
12. emphasized relevant concepts, themes, or ideas in instruction and assignments.					

Consensus Form
Consensus Form *The William and Mary Classroom Observation Scales, Revised (Part 2) Teacher Observation*
Joyce VanTassel-Baska, EdD Linda Avery, PhD   Jeanne Struck, PhD   Annie Feng, EdD Bruce Bracken, PhD   Dianne Drummond, MEd Tamra Stambaugh, MEd

Directions: Please employ the following scale as you rate each of the checklist items. Rate each item according to how well the teacher characteristic or behavior was demonstrated during the observed instructional activity. Each item is judged on an individual, self-contained basis, regardless of its relationship to an overall set of behaviors relevant to the cluster heading.

3 = Effective	2 = Somewhat Effective	1 = Ineffective	N/O = Not Observed
The teacher evidenced careful planning and classroom flexibility in implementation of the behavior, eliciting many appropriate student responses. The teacher was clear and sustained focus on the purposes of learning.	The teacher evidenced some planning and/or classroom flexibility in implementation of the behavior, eliciting some appropriate student responses. The teacher was sometimes clear and focused on the purposes of learning.	The teacher evidenced little or no planning and/or classroom flexibility in implementation of the behavior, eliciting minimal appropriate student responses. The teacher was unclear and unfocused regarding the purpose of learning.	The listed behavior was not demonstrated during the time of the observation. (NOTE: There must be an obvious attempt made for the certain behavior to be rated "ineffective" instead of "not observed.")

General Teaching Behaviors				
Curriculum Planning and Delivery	3	2	1	N/O
The teacher . . .				
1. set high expectations for student performance.				
2. incorporated activities for students to apply new knowledge.				
3. engaged students in planning, monitoring, or assessing their learning.				
4. encouraged students to express their thoughts.				
5. had students reflect on what they had learned.				
Comments:				

(Continued)

(Continued)

Differentiated Teaching Behaviors				
Accommodations for Individual Differences	3	2	1	N/O
The teacher . . .				
6. provided opportunities for independent or group learning to promote depth in understanding content.				
7. accommodated individual or subgroup differences (e.g., through individual conferencing, student or teacher choice in material selection, and task assignments.)				
8. encouraged multiple interpretations of events and situations.				
9. allowed students to discover key ideas individually through structured activities and/or questions.				
Comments:				
Problem Solving	3	2	1	N/O
The teacher . . .				
10. employed brainstorming techniques.				
11. engaged students in problem identification and definition.				
12. engaged students in solution-finding activities and comprehensive solution articulation.				
Comments:				
Critical Thinking Strategies	3	2	1	N/O
The teacher . . .				
13. encouraged students to judge or evaluate situations, problems, or issues.				
14. engaged students in comparing and contrasting ideas (e.g., analyze generated ideas).				
15. provided opportunities for students to generalize from concrete data or information to the abstract.				
16. encouraged student synthesis or summary of information within or across disciplines.				
Comments:				

Creative Thinking Strategies				
Accommodations for Individual Differences	*3*	*2*	*1*	*N/O*
The teacher . . .				
17. solicited many diverse thoughts about issues or ideas.				
18. engaged students in the exploration of diverse points of view to reframe ideas.				
19. encouraged students to demonstrate open-mindedness and tolerance of imaginative, sometimes playful solutions to problems.				
20. provided opportunities for students to develop and elaborate on their ideas.				
Comments:				

Research Strategies	*3*	*2*	*1*	*N/O*
(It is atypical for these to be observed in one session. Some teachers, however, may use Items 21–25 within a single period to illustrate the full research process to students. Please note those observations in the comments section.)				
The teacher . . .				
21. required students to gather evidence from multiple sources through research-based techniques (e.g., print, nonprint, Internet, self-investigation via surveys, interviews, etc.).				
22. provided opportunities for students to analyze data and represent it in appropriate charts, graphs, or tables.				
23. asked questions to assist students in making inferences from data and drawing conclusions.				
24. encouraged students to determine implications and consequences of findings.				
25. provided time for students to communicate research study findings to relevant audiences in a formal report and/or presentation.				
Comments:				

Additional Comments:

Consensus Form
The William and Mary Classroom Observation Scales, Revised (Part 3)
Student Observation

Joyce VanTassel-Baska, EdD   Bruce Bracken, PhD   Dianne Drummond, MEd

Student Responses to General Classroom Teacher Behaviors

Students:	Most	Many	Some	Few	None	N/A
26. demonstrated a high level of performance.						
27. applied new learning.						
28. demonstrated planful, monitoring, or evaluating behavior.						
29. articulated thinking process (e.g., verbal mediation).						
30. reflected on learning.						
Comments:						

Student Responses to Differentiated Teaching Behaviors

Engaged in Diverse Self-Selected or Self-Paced Activities Students:	Most	Many	Some	Few	None	N/A
31. worked on projects individually or in pairs/groups.						
32. worked on tiered assignments or tasks of choice.						
33. explored multiple interpretations.						
34. discovered central ideas through structured activities and/or questions asked.						
Comments:						

Engaged in Problem-Solving Strategies Students:	Most	Many	Some	Few	None	N/A
35. brainstormed ideas or alternative possibilities.						
36. defined problems.						
37. identified and implemented solutions to problems.						
Comments:						

Engaged in Critical Thinking Strategies Students:	Most	Many	Some	Few	None	N/A
38. made judgments about or evaluated situations, problems, or issues.						
39. compared and contrasted ideas and concepts.						
40. generalized from specific to abstract data or information.						
41. synthesized or summarized information within or across disciplines.						

Comments:

Engaged in Creative Thinking Strategies Students:	Most	Many	Some	Few	None	N/A
42. demonstrated ideational fluency.						
43. explored diverse ways to think about a situation/object/event.						
44. offered imaginative, sometimes playful, suggestions as solutions to problems.						
45. provided examples and illustrations of ideas.						

Comments:

Engaged in Research Strategies Students:	Most	Many	Some	Few	None	N/A
46. gathered evidence through research techniques (e.g., surveys, interviews, analysis of primary and secondary source documents).						
47. manipulated and transformed data to be interpreted.						
48. made inferences from data and drew conclusions.						
49. determined the implications and consequences of situations.						
50. communicated findings (e.g., report, oral presentation).						

Comments:

The William and Mary Classroom Observation Scales
Lesson Plan Script Sheet

What's Going On? (Methods and Organization)	Number of Minutes	Questions or Comments (Specific Quotes)		Other Observations (include number of students answering or involved)
		Teacher	Student	

Unanticipated Student Behaviors Observed:

The William and Mary Classroom Observation Scales
Lesson Plan Script Sheet (Continued)

What's Going On? (Methods and Organization)	Number of Minutes	Questions or Comments (Specific Quotes)		Other Observations (include number of students answering or involved)
		Teacher	Student	

Unanticipated Student Behaviors Observed:

The William and Mary Classroom Observation Scales
Lesson Plan Script Sheet (Continued)

What's Going On? (Methods and Organization)	Number of Minutes	Questions or Comments (Specific Quotes)		Other Observations (include number of students answering or involved)
		Teacher	**Student**	

Unanticipated Student Behaviors Observed:

William and Mary Classroom Observation Scales, Revised
Teacher Interview Form

Questions	Teacher Responses
Did you have a written lesson plan for this lesson?	____ yes ____ no
How would you characterize the purpose of the lesson?	
What were your instructional objectives for the previous lesson with this class?	
What content will you cover in your subsequent lesson?	
What plans do you have to address homework or extensions of this lesson?	
How do you intend to assess the outcomes for this lesson? Final outcomes for the unit?	
Are there any aspects of the lesson you would like to clarify before this observation is finalized?	

Source: Reprinted with permission from Center for Gifted Education, College of William and Mary.

PURDUE UNIVERSITY GIFTED EDUCATION RESOURCE INSTITUTE

Teacher Observation Form

Teacher _____ Date _____

Time _____ Location _____

Course _____ Grades (or Ages)_____

CATEGORY/CRITERIA: Ranking for each category is
determined by observation of one or more of the criteria listed below it.

1. Subject matter coverage
   A. Appropriateness of depth and breadth
   B. Concept orientation
   C. Teacher expertise

5	4	3	2	1	N/O

2. Clarity of teaching
   A. Verbal communication skills
   B. Nonverbal communication skills
   C. Clear and specific directions
   D. All necessary points addressed
   E. Sufficient illustrations and examples
      (e.g., use of analogies, similes, etc.)
   F. Student comprehension as evidenced
      by responses and involvement

3. Motivational techniques
   A. Teacher energy and enthusiasm
   B. Variety (warmups, brainteasers, etc.)
   C. Student enthusiasm and persistence demonstrated

4. Pace of instruction
   A. Individualized needs accommodated
   B. Appropriate for the group
   C. Avoidance of unnecessary repetition, drill, use of
      examples

**5. Opportunity for self-determination of
   activities by student**
   A. Adequate choices offered
   B. Student-directed activities
   C. Individual interests accommodated

6. Student involvement in a variety of experiences
   A. Discussions, small-group activities, movies, field
      trips, learning centers, etc.
   B. Purposeful use of movement
   C. Creative thinking, problem solving, independent study processes
   D. Learning style accommodation

	5	4	3	2	1	N/O

7. Interaction between teacher and student, student and peers, appropriate to course objectives

    A. Activities that promote group feeling

    B. Respect for individuals and their ideas

    C. Appropriate use of humor

    D. Sense of order promoting self-discipline

8. Opportunity for student follow-through of activities outside class (homework)

    A. Open-endedness, allowing for creativity and individual interests and pace

    B. Builds upon or prepares for classroom activities

    C. Variety of assignments

    D. Encouragement of and assistance in further study for interested students

    E. Handouts and instructions are clearly printed and thorough

RATING SCALE

5 -- Outstanding	2 -- Needs some improvement	____ - Criteria observed
4 -- High	1 -- Not satisfactory	____ - Criteria not observed
3 -- Average	N/O - Not Observed	

9. Emphasis on higher-level thinking skills

    _____ A. Bloom's Taxonomy evidenced in teacher questioning, activities, teaching aids

    _____ B. Critical thinking activities (e.g., logic, simulations, scientific process)

10. Emphasis on creativity

    _____ A. Creative thinking skills (fluency, flexibility, originality, elaboration)

    _____ B. Accepting atmosphere

    _____ C. Encouragement of risk taking

    _____ D. Open-ended questioning

    _____ E. Models creative behavior

11. Lesson plans designed to meet program, course, and daily objectives

    _____ A. Sense of planning with flexibility

    _____ B. Student centered

12. Use of teaching and learning aids

    _____ A. Inclusion of audio-visual materials, models, demonstrations, etc.

    _____ B. Clearly printed and grammatically correct

    _____ C. Appropriate/necessary

    _____ D. Variety of materials/aids used

Activities were conducted in _____ small groups _____ large groups _____ individually.

(Continued)

(Continued)
_____

Teacher's strengths:
_____
_____
_____
_____
_____
_____

Suggestions for improvement:
_____
_____
_____
_____
_____

Additional comments:
_____
_____
_____
_____
_____
_____

Observer's Signature:_____

Review by Teacher: _____ Date: _____

☐ Would like conference regarding evaluation.   Suggested time:_____

Source: Reprinted with permission from Hansen & Feldhusen (1994).

Appendix B

Needs Assessments

Sample Needs Assessment Survey

(addressing needs, interests, drivers, and perceived obstacles)

1. Currently, what is your *primary* position?
   a. Elementary teacher
   b. Middle school teacher (indicate subjects) _____
   c. High school teacher (indicate subjects) _____
   d. Administrator

2. What is your current teaching assignment? Check all that apply.
   a. Gifted cluster
   b. Gifted self-contained
   c. Advanced Placement/Honors
   d. International Baccalaureate
   e. General education classroom
   f. Other (please specify) _____
   g. I have no teaching assignment.

3. Have you participated in any of the following? Check all that apply.
   a. District's professional development program in gifted education
   b. Distinguished lectures offered by GATE office
   c. Professional conferences on gifted education or Advanced Placement
   d. Reading professional literature in gifted education

4. Do you adapt your curriculum and instruction for the learning needs of gifted students? (If you are an administrator, do you encourage teachers to adapt?)
   a. Yes, extensively
   b. Yes, somewhat
   c. Minimally
   d. Not at all

5. Based on results of formal and informal assessments of your students' performance, what do you perceive as areas requiring support? Check all that apply.
   a. Critical thinking
   b. Problem solving
   c. Metacognition
   d. Creative thinking
   e. English language development
   f. Social/emotional development
   g. Positive coping strategies and self-efficacy
   h. Rigor in a content area (please specify) _____
   i. Other (please specify) _____

6. Do you currently use any of the following strategies to accommodate the learning needs of gifted and talented students? Check all that apply. (Administrators: do you encourage teachers to use any of the following?)
   a. Engaging students in powerful discussions (e.g., Socratic seminars)
   b. Curriculum compacting
   c. Providing optimal levels of challenge and rigor
   d. Problem-based learning
   e. Independent projects
   f. Tiered assignments based on student readiness level
   g. Challenging multicultural curriculum and culturally consonant instruction
   h. Choices; opportunities to pursue interests/passions
   i. Opportunities to move ahead in the curriculum
   j. Engagement in higher-level thinking (e.g., synthesis, critical thinking)
   k. Opportunities for inquiry and research
   l. Engagement in real-life topics
   m. Opportunities for creative productivity
   n. Development of authentic products (for real audiences)
   o. Support for social and emotional development
   p. Connecting students with mentors
   q. Other (please specify) _____

7. If you implement any of the above strategies, what has been the impact on students? Check all that apply.
   a. Increased engagement or motivation
   b. Increased knowledge and skills
   c. Higher-level or creative thinking
   d. Other (please specify) _____
   e. No detectible impact
   f. I do not implement any of the above strategies.

8. How confident are you in implementing these strategies?

   Very Confident (VC)   Somewhat Confident (SC)   Not Confident (NC)
   I don't implement this strategy (DI)

a. Powerful discussions	VC SC NC DI
b. Curriculum compacting	VC SC NC DI
c. Optimal levels of challenge & rigor	VC SC NC DI
d. Problem-based learning	VC SC NC DI
e. Independent projects	VC SC NC DI

f. Tiered assignments	VC	SC	NC	DI
g. Challenging multicultural curriculum and instruction	VC	SC	NC	DI
h. Choices; opportunities to pursue interests/passions	VC	SC	NC	DI
i. Opportunities to move ahead in the curriculum	VC	SC	NC	DI
j. Engagement in higher-level thinking	VC	SC	NC	DI
k. Opportunities for inquiry and research	VC	SC	NC	DI
l. Engagement in real-life topics	VC	SC	NC	DI
m. Opportunities for creative productivity	VC	SC	NC	DI
n. Development of authentic products (for real audiences)	VC	SC	NC	DI
o. Support for social and emotional development	VC	SC	NC	DI
p. Connecting students with mentors	VC	SC	NC	DI
q. Other (please specify)	VC	SC	NC	DI

9. What factors have supported or would likely support your implementation of strategies for differentiating instruction? Check all that apply.
   a. Attending conferences and workshops
   b. Continuing professional development offered by the district
   c. Coaching
   d. Observing master teachers of the gifted
   e. Principal support
   f. Other (please specify) _____

10. What factors have discouraged or limited implementation? Check all that apply.
    a. Range of student needs
    b. Insufficient training
    c. Lack of site support
    d. Lack of materials or other resources
    e. Incompatibility with curriculum or standards
    f. Other (please specify) _____

11. Professional development in gifted education is required each year. Please indicate the topics that would most interest you.

    _____

12. Would you be interested in any of the following opportunities to share your expertise? Check all that apply:
    a. Providing a workshop
    b. Serving as a demonstration teacher
    c. Other leadership role (please specify) _____

    If you would like to be contacted about these opportunities, you may write your name in the comments section; doing so would eliminate anonymity.

13. Any comments or suggestions for improving the district's professional development offerings?

    Thank you for completing the survey.

NAGC – CEC Teacher Knowledge and Skill Standards for Gifted and Talented Education

Please assess your status on each knowledge and skill statement, as follows:

ADVANCED	PROFICIENT	BASIC	BEGINNING	NOT YET BEGUN
5	**4**	**3**	**2**	**1**

STANDARD 1: FOUNDATIONS

Educators of the gifted understand the field as an evolving and changing discipline based on philosophies, evidence-based principles and theories, relevant laws and policies, diverse and historical points of view, and human issues. These perspectives continue to influence the field of gifted education and the education and treatment of individuals with gifts and talents both in school and society. They recognize how foundational influences affect professional practice, including assessment, instructional planning, delivery, and program evaluation. They further understand how issues of human diversity impact families, cultures, and schools, and how these complex human issues can interact in the delivery of gifted and talented education services.

K1	Historical foundations of gifted and talented education, including points of view and contributions of individuals from diverse backgrounds.	5 4 3 2 1
K2	Key philosophies, theories, models, and research that supports gifted and talented education.	5 4 3 2 1
K3	Local, state/provincial, and federal laws and policies related to gifted and talented education.	5 4 3 2 1
K4	Issues in conceptions, definitions, and identification of individuals with gifts and talents, including those of individuals from diverse backgrounds.	5 4 3 2 1
K5	Impact of the dominant culture's role in shaping schools and the differences in values, languages, and customs between school and home.	5 4 3 2 1
K6	Societal, cultural, and economic factors, including anti-intellectualism and equity versus excellence, enhancing or inhibiting the development of gifts and talents.	5 4 3 2 1
K7	Key issues and trends, including diversity and inclusion, that connect general, special, and gifted and talented education.	5 4 3 2 1

STANDARD 2: DEVELOPMENT AND CHARACTERISTICS OF LEARNERS

Educators of the gifted know and demonstrate respect for their students as unique human beings. They understand variations in characteristics and development between and among individuals with and without exceptional learning needs and capacities. Educators of the gifted can express how different characteristics interact with the domains of human development and use this knowledge to describe the varying abilities and behaviors of individuals with gifts and talents. Educators of the gifted also understand how families and communities contribute to the development of individuals with gifts and talents.

K1	Cognitive and affective characteristics of individuals with gifts and talents, including those from diverse backgrounds, in intellectual, academic, creative, leadership, and artistic domains.	5 4 3 2 1
K2	Characteristics and effects of culture and environment on the development of individuals with gifts and talents.	5 4 3 2 1
K3	Role of families and communities in supporting the development of individuals with gifts and talents.	5 4 3 2 1
K4	Advanced developmental milestones of individuals with gifts and talents from early childhood through adolescence.	5 4 3 2 1
K5	Similarities and differences within the group of individuals with gifts and talents as compared to the general population.	5 4 3 2 1

STANDARD 3: INDIVIDUAL LEARNING DIFFERENCES

Educators of the gifted understand the effects that gifts and talents can have on an individual's learning in school and throughout life. Moreover, educators of the gifted are active and resourceful in seeking to understand how language, culture, and family background interact with an individual's predispositions to impact academic and social behavior, attitudes, values, and interests. The understanding of these learning differences and their interactions provides the foundation upon which educators of the gifted plan instruction to provide meaningful and challenging learning.

K1	Influences of diversity factors on individuals with gifts and talents.	5 4 3 2 1
K2	Academic and affective characteristics and learning needs of individuals with gifts, talents, and disabilities.	5 4 3 2 1
K3	Idiosyncratic learning patterns of individuals with gifts and talents, including those from diverse backgrounds.	5 4 3 2 1
K4	Influences of different beliefs, traditions, and values across and within diverse groups on relationships among individuals with gifts and talents, their families, schools, and communities.	5 4 3 2 1
S1	Integrate perspectives of diverse groups into planning instruction for individuals with gifts and talents.	5 4 3 2 1

STANDARD 4: INSTRUCTIONAL STRATEGIES

Educators of the gifted possess a repertoire of evidence-based curriculum and instructional strategies to differentiate for individuals with gifts and talents. They select, adapt, and use these strategies to promote challenging learning opportunities in general and special curricula and to modify learning environments to enhance self-awareness and self-efficacy for individuals with gifts and talents. They enhance the learning of critical and creative thinking, problem solving, and performance skills in specific domains. Moreover, educators of the gifted emphasize the development, practice, and transfer of advanced knowledge and skills across environments throughout the life span leading to creative, productive careers in society for individuals with gifts and talents.

K1	School and community resources, including content specialists, that support differentiation.	5 4 3 2 1
K2	Curricular, instructional, and management strategies effective for individuals with exceptional learning needs.	5 4 3 2 1
S1	Apply pedagogical content knowledge to instructing learners with gifts and talents.	5 4 3 2 1
S2	Apply higher-level thinking and metacognitive models to content areas to meet the needs of individuals with gifts and talents.	5 4 3 2 1
S3	Provide opportunities for individuals with gifts and talents to explore, develop, or research their areas of interest or talent.	5 4 3 2 1
S4	Preassess the learning needs of individuals with gifts and talents in various domains and adjust instruction based on continual assessment.	5 4 3 2 1
S5	Pace delivery of curriculum and instruction consistent with needs of individuals with gifts and talents.	5 4 3 2 1
S6	Engage individuals with gifts and talents from all backgrounds in challenging, multicultural curricula.	5 4 3 2 1
S7	Use information and/or assistive technologies to meet the needs of individuals with exceptional learning needs.	5 4 3 2 1

STANDARD 5: LEARNING ENVIRONMENTS AND SOCIAL INTERACTIONS

Educators of the gifted actively create learning environments for individuals with gifts and talents that foster cultural understanding, safety and emotional well-being, positive social interactions, and active engagement. In addition, educators of the gifted foster environments in which diversity is valued and individuals are taught to live harmoniously and productively in a culturally diverse world. Educators of the gifted shape environments to encourage independence, motivation, and self-advocacy of individuals with gifts and talents.

K1	Ways in which groups are stereotyped and experience historical and current discrimination and implications for gifted and talented education.	5 4 3 2 1
K2	Influence of social and emotional development on interpersonal relationships and learning of individuals with gifts and talents.	5 4 3 2 1
S1	Design learning opportunities for individuals with gifts and talents that promote self-awareness, positive peer relationships, intercultural experiences, and leadership.	5 4 3 2 1
S2	Create learning environments for individuals with gifts and talents that promote self-awareness, self-efficacy, leadership, and lifelong learning.	5 4 3 2 1
S3	Create safe learning environments for individuals with gifts and talents that encourage active participation in individual and group activities to enhance independence, interdependence, and positive peer relationships.	5 4 3 2 1
S4	Create learning environments and intercultural experiences that allow individuals with gifts and talents to appreciate their own and others' language and cultural heritage.	5 4 3 2 1
S5	Develop social interaction and coping skills in individuals with gifts and talents to address personal and social issues, including discrimination and stereotyping.	5 4 3 2 1

STANDARD 6: LANGUAGE AND COMMUNICATION

Educators of the gifted understand the role of language and communication in talent development and the ways in which exceptional conditions can hinder or facilitate such development. They use relevant strategies to teach oral and written communication skills to individuals with gifts and talents. Educators of the gifted are familiar with assistive technologies to support and enhance communication of individuals with exceptional needs. They match their communication methods to an individual's language proficiency and cultural and linguistic differences. Educators of the gifted use communication strategies and resources to facilitate understanding of subject matter for individuals with gifts and talents who are English language learners.

K1	Forms and methods of communication essential to the education of individuals with gifts and talents, including those from diverse backgrounds.	5 4 3 2 1
K2	Impact of diversity on communication.	5 4 3 2 1
K3	Implications of culture, behavior, and language on the development of individuals with gifts and talents.	5 4 3 2 1
S1	Access resources and develop strategies to enhance communication skills for individuals with gifts and talents, including those with advanced communication and/or English language learners.	5 4 3 2 1
S2	Use advanced oral and written communication tools, including assistive technologies, to enhance the learning experiences of individuals with exceptional learning needs.	5 4 3 2 1

STANDARD 7: INSTRUCTIONAL PLANNING

Curriculum and instructional planning is at the center of gifted and talented education. Educators of the gifted develop long-range plans anchored in both general and special curricula. They systematically translate shorter-range goals and objectives that take into consideration an individual's abilities and needs, the learning environment, and cultural and linguistic factors. Understanding of these factors, as well as the implications of being gifted and talented, guides the educator's selection, adaptation, and creation of materials, and use of differentiated instructional strategies. Learning plans are modified based on ongoing assessment of the individual's progress. Moreover, educators of the gifted facilitate these actions in a collaborative context that includes individuals with gifts and talents, families, professional colleagues, and personnel from other agencies as appropriate. Educators of the gifted are comfortable using technologies to support instructional planning and individualized instruction.

K1	Theories and research models that form the basis of curriculum development and instructional practice for individuals with gifts and talents.	5 4 3 2 1
K2	Features that distinguish differentiated curriculum from general curricula for individuals with exceptional learning needs.	5 4 3 2 1
K3	Curriculum emphases for individuals with gifts and talents within cognitive, affective, aesthetic, social, and linguistic domains.	5 4 3 2 1
S1	Align differentiated instructional plans with local, state/provincial, and national curricular standards.	5 4 3 2 1
S2	Design differentiated learning plans for individuals with gifts and talents, including individuals from diverse backgrounds.	5 4 3 2 1
S3	Develop scope and sequence plans for individuals with gifts and talents.	5 4 3 2 1
S4	Select curriculum resources, strategies, and product options that respond to cultural, linguistic, and intellectual differences among individuals with gifts and talents.	5 4 3 2 1
S5	Select and adapt a variety of differentiated curricula that incorporate advanced, conceptually challenging, in-depth, distinctive, and complex content.	5 4 3 2 1
S6	Integrate academic and career guidance experiences into the learning plan for individuals with gifts and talents.	5 4 3 2 1

STANDARD 8: ASSESSMENT

Assessment is integral to the decision making and teaching of educators of the gifted as multiple types of assessment information are required for both identification and learning progress decisions. Educators of the gifted use the results of such assessments to adjust instruction and to enhance ongoing learning progress. Educators of the gifted understand the process of identification, legal policies, and ethical principles of measurement and assessment related to referral, eligibility, program planning, instruction, and placement for individuals with gifts and talents, including those from culturally and linguistically diverse backgrounds. They understand measurement theory and practices for addressing the interpretation of assessment results. In addition, educators of the gifted understand the appropriate use and limitations of various types of assessments. To ensure the use of nonbiased and equitable identification and learning progress models, educators of the gifted employ alternative assessments such as performance-based assessment, portfolios, and computer simulations.

K1	Processes and procedures for the identification of individuals with gifts and talents.	5 4 3 2 1
K2	Uses, limitations, and interpretation of multiple assessments in different domains for identifying individuals with exceptional learning needs, including those from diverse backgrounds.	5 4 3 2 1
K3	Uses and limitations of assessments documenting academic growth of individuals with gifts and talents.	5 4 3 2 1
S1	Use nonbiased and equitable approaches for identifying individuals with gifts and talents, including those from diverse backgrounds.	5 4 3 2 1
S2	Use technically adequate qualitative and quantitative assessments for identifying and placing individuals with gifts and talents.	5 4 3 2 1
S3	Develop differentiated curriculum-based assessments for use in instructional planning and delivery for individuals with gifts and talents.	5 4 3 2 1
S4	Use alternative assessments and technologies to evaluate learning of individuals with gifts and talents.	5 4 3 2 1

STANDARD 9: PROFESSIONAL AND ETHICAL PRACTICE

Educators of the gifted are guided by the profession's ethical and professional practice standards. They practice in multiple roles and complex situations across wide age and developmental ranges. Their practice requires ongoing attention to professional and ethical considerations. They engage in professional activities that promote growth in individuals with gifts and talents and update themselves on evidence-based best practices. Educators of the gifted view themselves as lifelong learners and regularly reflect on and adjust their practice. They are aware of how attitudes, behaviors, and ways of communicating can influence their practice. Educators of the gifted understand that culture and language interact with gifts and talents and are sensitive to the many aspects of the diversity of individuals with gifts and talents and their families.

K1	Personal and cultural frames of reference that affect one's teaching of individuals with gifts and talents, including biases about individuals from diverse backgrounds.	5 4 3 2 1
K2	Organizations and publications relevant to the field of gifted and talented education.	5 4 3 2 1
S1	Assess personal skills and limitations in teaching individuals with exceptional learning needs.	5 4 3 2 1
S2	Maintain confidential communication about individuals with gifts and talents.	5 4 3 2 1

S3	Encourage and model respect for the full range of diversity among individuals with gifts and talents.	5 4 3 2 1
S4	Conduct activities in gifted and talented education in compliance with laws, policies, and standards of ethical practice.	5 4 3 2 1
S5	Improve practice through continuous research-supported professional development in gifted education and related fields.	5 4 3 2 1
S6	Participate in the activities of professional organizations related to gifted and talented education.	5 4 3 2 1
S7	Reflect on personal practice to improve teaching and guide professional growth in gifted and talented education.	5 4 3 2 1

STANDARD 10: COLLABORATION

Educators of the gifted effectively collaborate with families, other educators, and related service providers. This collaboration enhances comprehensive articulated program options across educational levels and engagement of individuals with gifts and talents in meaningful learning activities and interactions. Moreover, educators of the gifted embrace their special role as advocate for individuals with gifts and talents. They promote and advocate for the learning and well-being of individuals with gifts and talents across settings and diverse learning experiences.

K1	Culturally responsive behaviors that promote effective communication and collaboration with individuals with gifts and talents, their families, school personnel, and community members.	5 4 3 2 1
S1	Respond to concerns of families of individuals with gifts and talents.	5 4 3 2 1
S2	Collaborate with stakeholders outside the school setting who serve individuals with exceptional learning needs and their families.	5 4 3 2 1
S3	Advocate for the benefit of individuals with gifts and talents and their families.	5 4 3 2 1
S4	Collaborate with individuals with gifts and talents, their families, general and special educators, and other school staff to articulate a comprehensive preschool through secondary educational program.	5 4 3 2 1
S5	Collaborate with families, community members, and professionals in assessment of individuals with gifts and talents.	5 4 3 2 1
S6	Communicate and consult with school personnel about the characteristics and needs of individuals with gifts and talents, including individuals from diverse backgrounds.	5 4 3 2 1

Appendix C

Sample Professional Development Plan for Teachers of the Gifted and Talented

Name _____ Date _____

School _____

Describing Your Professional Development Goal

1. What is your professional development goal for the coming academic year?

2. How did you determine the need for this goal?

3. How will achievement of this goal affect you? Your students' achievement or development?

Relationship of Goal to Standards

4. How does the goal relate to the national standards for entry-level teachers of the gifted?

5. How does the goal relate to standards for programs serving the gifted and talented?

Evaluating Outcomes and Sharing With Others

6. What will be the outcome or product? How will the outcome or product be evaluated, including impact on students?

7. How will you disseminate what you have learned and to what audiences?

(Continued)

(Continued)

Resources Needed

8. What resources or support will you need (e.g., from district, principal, colleagues)?

9. What objectives and activities will enable the accomplishment of your goal?

Objective	Activity	Timeline

Appendix D

Sample Assessment Rubric: Multicultural Literature Unit

Developed by M. Kitano, San Diego State University

Gifted & Talented K&S	Proficient	Competent	Developing
Planning • 1K2 key philosophies, theories, models, research • 3S1 perspectives of diverse groups in planning instruction • 10K1 culturally responsive behaviors promoting communication with families	• Explicitly based on key philosophies, theories, models, and/or research • Is designed for consistency with developmental expectations for gifted • Includes culturally appropriate communication with and involvement of families	• Does not explicitly consider but is consistent with key philosophies, theories, models, or research • Is consistent with developmental expectations for gifted • Families are consulted	• Does not consider key philosophies, theories, models, or research • Is partially consistent with developmental expectations for gifted • Families are not consulted
Objectives of Unit • 7S1 align with local, state, national curricular standards	• Are consistent with identified unit theme • Reflect appropriate levels of challenge and accommodate diverse learners (e.g., EL gifted) • Are consistent with and go beyond district's essential questions	• Are consistent with identified unit theme • Reflect appropriate levels of challenge for gifted • Are consistent with district essential questions and go beyond for gifted	• Are consistent with identified unit theme • Within students' range but not challenging • Are consistent with district's essential questions
Preassessment • 4S4 preassess learning needs	• Identifies individual student status on objectives • Data are used to determine differentiated learning activities	• Identifies group status on objectives • Data are used to determine learning activities	• Not conducted or data are not used for determining activities

(Continued)

(Continued)

Gifted & Talented K&S	Proficient	Competent	Developing
Selection of Literature • 4S6 challenging multicultural curricula • 5K1 ways groups are stereotyped and experience historical and current discrimination • 5K2 influence of social and emotional development • 5S1 design opportunities that promote self-efficacy • 7S4 select resources that respond to cultural, linguistic, intellectual differences	• Engages students in target issues (for this example: coping strategies, moral courage, multiple perspectives, historical and current discrimination) • Reflects students' diversity in respectful and authentic ways • Presents historical look at discrimination and continuation into present time	• Engages students in some of the target issues • Reflects some students' diversity and in respectful ways; critically analyzes any stereotypical views • Presents discrimination as a historical issue	• Minimally engages students in target issues • Reflects students' diversity minimally and in stereotypical ways without critical analysis • Ignores discrimination as an issue
Instructional Activities • 4S2 higher-level thinking • 5S2 safe learning environments • 5S3 intercultural experiences • 5S4 social interactions and coping skills to address personal and social issues, including discrimination and stereotyping • 7S5 advanced, conceptually challenging content • 9S3 encourage and model respect for diversity	• Support student achievement of objectives • Provide appropriate challenge and accommodation for diverse needs • Engage students in higher-level thinking • Reinforce metacognitive strategies for confronting social issues • Explicitly teach requesting of peers' ideas and using respectful ways to disagree • Engage teacher in modeling respect for diversity	• Support student achievement of some of the objectives • Differentiate only for gifted • Engage some students in higher-level thinking • Avoid difficult social issues • Offer minimal guidance to encourage respectful peer interactions • Engage teacher in modeling respect for diversity	• Support student achievement of one objective • Use same activity and level of scaffolding for all • Do not provide opportunities for higher-level thinking • Avoid or ignore difficult social issues • No guidance and monitoring for respectful peer interactions
Evaluation • 8S3 develop differentiated curriculum-based assessments	• Assessments provide data indicating individual status on objectives • Data guide revisions	• Assessments provide data indicating groups' status on objectives • Data guide revisions	• Assessments not implemented or data are not used to guide reflection and change

Appendix E

Sample Concept Maps

Concept Map Key

Adapted from: Novak, J., & Gowin, D. (1984). *Learning how to learn*. Cambridge, UK: Cambridge University Press.

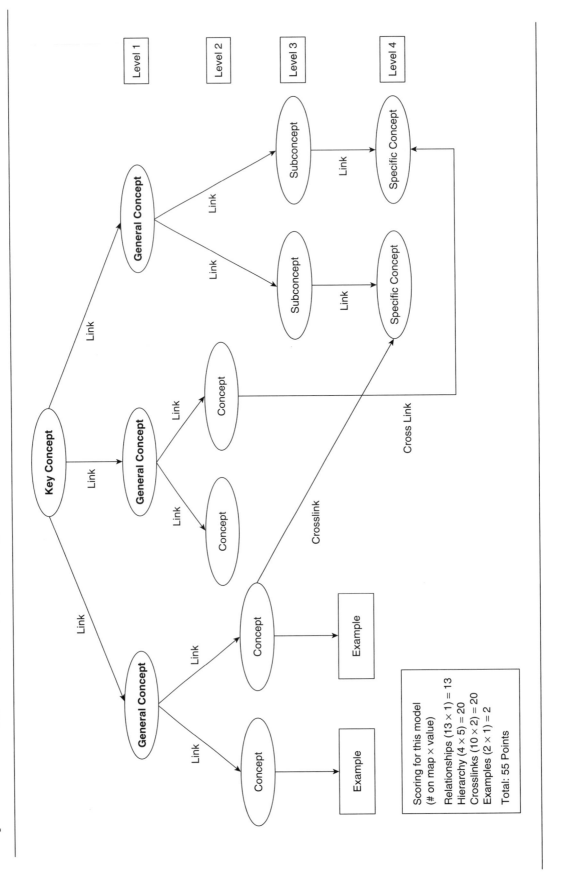

Map 1

Name: Intern 1

Date: 8/23/04

You will have 45 minutes to construct a concept map about effective teaching for students with gifts and talents. In the center of this page, draw a circle that says, "effective teaching for GT students." Draw spokes from this circle and label those. From these smaller circles, draw other smaller circles until you are satisfied with your map. At the end of 45 minutes you will have 15 minutes to explain the reasons for selecting the categories and subcategories on the back or on a separate sheet of paper if you need more room.

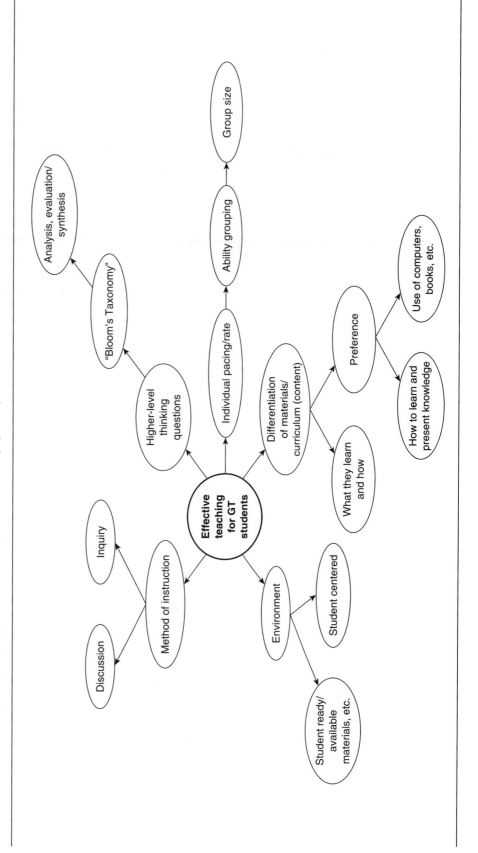

Rationale:

Higher-level thinking questions: Bloom's is a method to dig into the content of a subject, and there are three levels of questioning, each one going deeper into the meaning. The questioning techniques help students find out more information that is not face value.

Pacing rate: Each student should be able to work at the rate at which he or she needs to intake the most knowledge. Not all students work at the same pace. Grouping can help with this concept. Ability grouping is good for students because it keeps them from being too bored or being challenged too much.

Differentiation: This can be done in all classrooms, and it helps cater to the needs of all students. It can be a totally different concept they learn or just a specific concept presented at a higher level.

Preference: This deals with how students choose to learn a concept, which is related to method of instruction—learning by inquiry and self-discovery rather than just teacher instruction/discussion. Preference is also related to the materials they use to learn: books, magazines, computers, etc.

Environment: It is good to have an independent-style classroom where the children take responsibility for their learning; students initiate their learning, and the classroom is set up to be child-centered and friendly use of materials is available.

Concept Map 1, Scored

Name: Intern 1

Date: 8/23/04

You will have 45 minutes to construct a concept map about effective teaching for students with gifts and talents. In the center of this page, draw a circle that says, "effective teaching for GT students." Draw spokes from this circle and label those. From these smaller circles, draw other smaller circles until you are satisfied with your map. At the end of 45 minutes you will have 15 minutes to explain the reasons for selecting the categories and subcategories on the back or on a separate sheet of paper if you need more room.

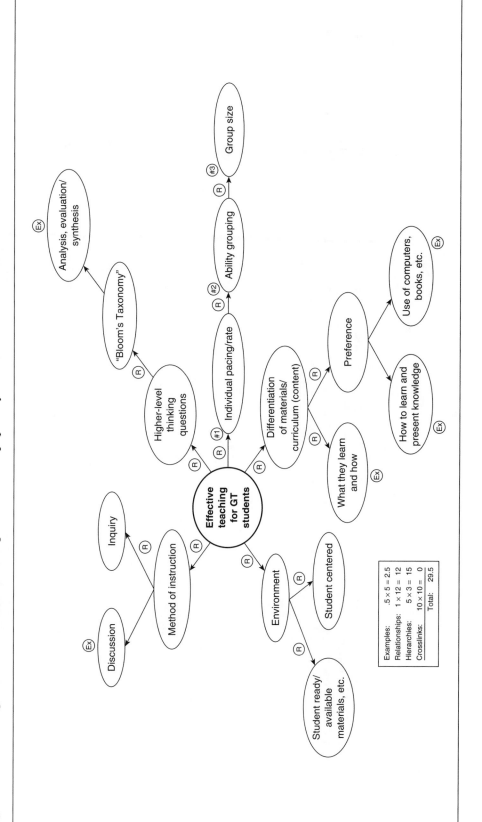

Map 3

Name: Intern 1

Date: 3/29/05

You will have 45 minutes to construct a concept map about effective teaching for students with gifts and talents. In the center of this page, draw a circle that says, "effective teaching for GT students." Draw spokes from this circle and label those. From these smaller circles, draw other smaller circles until you are satisfied with your map. At the end of 45 minutes you will have 15 minutes to explain the reasons for selecting the categories and subcategories on the back or on a separate sheet of paper if you need more room.

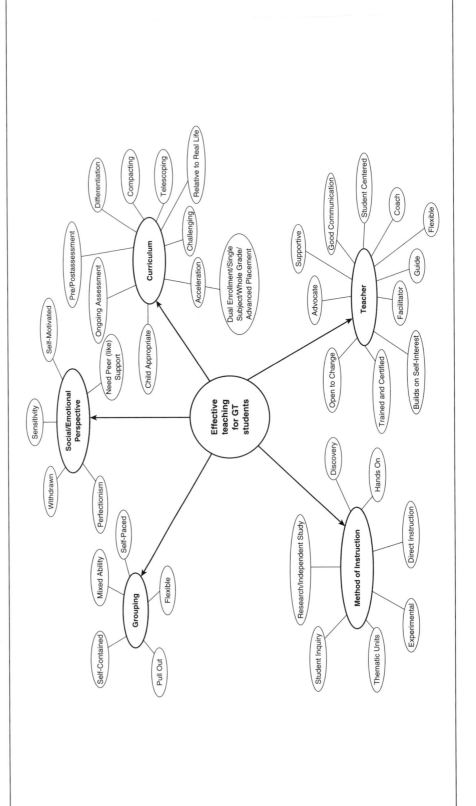

Rationale:

Curriculum: It is important to have curriculum that is child appropriate and that is individualized to meet the needs of each student. Allowing for self-pacing and differentiation to occur is very important for a student to stay interested and involved. Teachers should be flexible with what is being taught and should also strive to connect instruction to real-life experience, which will benefit the child outside the classroom.

Social/Emotional: GT kids have differences that cause them to look at life and their achievements differently; they need to have a safe peer group that they feel comfortable with and that understands and appreciates their differences.

Grouping: Flexibility is key! GT kids should be grouped with like ability and at times mixed, to benefit socially. Building upon their giftedness while at the same time their social growth is important.

Method of Instruction: It is very important for GT students to take ownership of their learning and discover new knowledge on their own. Exploration helps students to really grasp concepts, and hands-on learning is beneficial long-term.

Teacher: The teachers of GT students should be well equipped and trained. They should understand what GT is all about and how to best challenge students. Allowing for differences is good, and being flexible is key. Teachers should serve as advocates for them so they can reach their highest learning potential.

Concept Map 3, Scored

Name: Intern 1

Date: 3/29/05

You will have 45 minutes to construct a concept map about effective teaching for students with gifts and talents. In the center of this page, draw a circle that says, "effective teaching for GT students." Draw spokes from this circle and label those. From these smaller circles, draw other smaller circles until you are satisfied with your map. At the end of 45 minutes you will have 15 minutes to explain the reasons for selecting the categories and subcategories on the back or on a separate sheet of paper if you need more room.

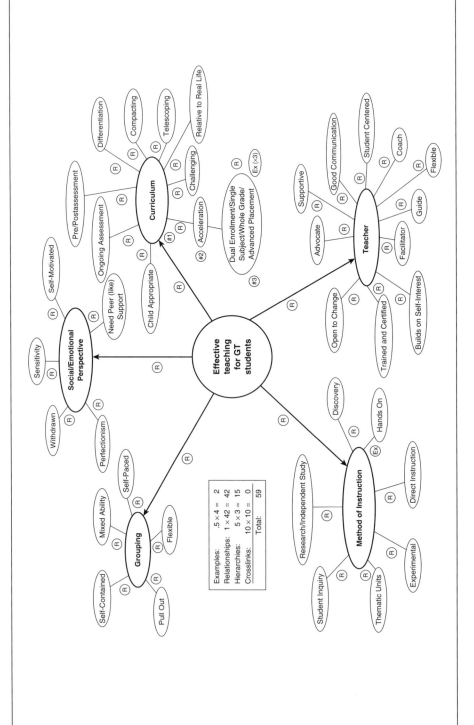

References

Ablard, K. E., & Tissot, S. L. (1998). Young students' readiness for advanced math: Precocious abstract reasoning. *Journal for the Education of the Gifted, 21*, 206–223.

Adams, C. M., & Pierce, R. L. (2003). Teaching by tiering. *Science & Children, 41*(3), 30–34.

Albert, R. S. (1996). What the study of eminence can teach us. *Creativity Research Journal, 9*, 307–315.

Albert, R., & Runco, M. (1989). Independence and the creative potential of gifted and exceptionally gifted boys. *Journal of Youth and Adolescence, 18*, 221–230.

Anderson, L. W., & Krathwohl, D. (Eds.). (2001). *A taxonomy for learning, teaching, and assessing: A revision of Bloom's taxonomy of educational objectives.* New York: Longman.

Artiles, A. J., & Zamora-Duran, G. (Eds.). (1997). *Reducing disproportionate representation of culturally diverse students in special and gifted education.* Arlington, VA: Council for Exceptional Children.

Association for the Gifted, The. (1989). *Standards for programs involving the gifted and talented.* Reston, VA: Council for Exceptional Children.

Association for the Gifted, The. (2001). *Diversity and developing gifts and talents: A national action plan.* Reston, VA: Council for Exceptional Children. (Available at www.gifted.uconn.edu/siegle/TAG/TAGBook.pdf)

Avery, L. D., VanTassel-Baska, J., & O'Neill, B. (1997). Making evaluation work: One school district's model. *Gifted Child Quarterly, 41*, 28–37.

Bain, S., Bourgeois, S., & Pappas, D. (2003). Linking theoretical models to actual practices: A survey of teachers in gifted education. *Roeper Review, 25*, 166–172.

Baldwin, A. Y. (2002). Culturally diverse students who are gifted. *Exceptionality, 10*, 139–147.

Barkan, J. H., & Bernal, E. M. (1991). Gifted education for bilingual and limited English proficient students. *Gifted Child Quarterly, 35*, 144–147.

Baum, S. M., Renzulli, J. S., & Hébert, T. P. (1995). Reversing underachievement: Creative productivity as a systematic intervention. *Gifted Child Quarterly, 39*, 224–235.

Belcher, R., & Fletcher-Carter, R. (1999). Growing gifted students in the desert: Using alternative, community-based assessment and an enriched curriculum. *Teaching Exceptional Children, 32*, 17–24.

Benbow, C. P., Lubinski, D., Shea, D. L., & Eftekhari-Sanjani, H. (2000). Sex differences in mathematical reasoning ability at age 13: Their status 20 years later. *Psychological Science. 11*, 474–480.

Bernal, E. M. (2002). Recruiting teachers for bilingual gifted and talented programs. In J. A. Castellano & E. I. Diaz (Eds.), *Reaching new horizons: Gifted and talented education for culturally and linguistically diverse students* (pp. 237–249). Boston: Allyn & Bacon.

Betts, G. (2004). Fostering autonomous learners through levels of differentiation. *Roeper Review, 26*, 190–191.

Betts, G. T., & Neihart, M. (1986). Implementing self-directed learning models for the gifted and talented. *Gifted Child Quarterly, 30*, 174–177.

Bloom, B. S. (Ed.). (1985). *Developing talent in young people.* New York: Ballantine.

Boothe, D., Sethna, B., Stanley, J. C., & Colgate, S. (1999). Special opportunities for exceptionally able high school students: A description of eight residential early-college entrance programs. *Journal of Secondary Gifted Education, 10*, 195–202.

Boothe, D., & Stanley, J. C. (Eds.). (2004). *In the eyes of the beholder: Critical issues for diversity in gifted education.* Waco, TX: Prufrock Press.

Borland, J. H., & Wright, L. (1994). Identifying young, potentially gifted, economically disadvantaged students. *Gifted Child Quarterly, 38*, 164–171.

Brody, L. (1999). The talent searches: Counseling and mentoring activities. In N. Colangelo & S. Assouline (Eds.), *Talent development III: Proceedings from the 1995 Henry B. and Jocelyn Wallace National Research Symposium on Talent Development* (pp. 153–157). Scottsdale, AZ: Great Potential Press.

Callahan, C., Cooper, C., & Glascock, R. (2003). *Preparing teachers to develop and enhance talent: The position of national education organizations.* (ERIC Document Services No. ED477882)

Cassady, J., Neumeister, K., Adams, C., Cross, T., Dixon, F., & Pierce, R. (2004). The differentiated classroom observation scale. *Roeper Review, 26*, 139–146.

Castellano, J. A. (2003). *Special populations in gifted education: Working with diverse gifted learners.* Boston: Allyn & Bacon.

Castellano, J. A., & Diaz, E. I. (Eds.). (2002). *Reaching new horizons: Gifted and talented education for culturally and linguistically diverse students.* Boston: Allyn & Bacon.

Castillo, L. C. (1998). The effect of analogy instruction on young children's metaphor comprehension. *Roeper Review, 21*, 27–31.

Cattell, R. B. (1963). Theory of fluid and crystallized intelligence: A critical experiment. *Journal of Educational Psychology, 54*, 1–22.

Cattell, R. B. (1971). *Abilities: Their structure, growth and action.* Boston: Houghton Mifflin.

Cazden, C. B., & Mehan, H. (1989). Principles from sociology and anthropology: Context, code, classroom and culture. In M. C. Reynolds (Ed.), *Knowledge base for the beginning teacher* (pp. 42–57). Oxford: Pergamon.

Center for Gifted Education. (2000). *Center for Gifted Education research model.* Williamsburg, VA: Author.

Choi, E. Y. (1998). Through another's eyes: Student fear number one. *Gifted Child Today, 21*(4), 30–31, 48.

Christophersen, E., & Mortweet, S. (2003). Encouraging independent play skills. In R. Christophersen & S. Mortweet (Eds.), *Parenting that works: Building skills that last a lifetime* (pp. 195–205). Washington, DC: American Psychological Association.

Clark, G. (2004). Screening and identifying students talented in the visual arts: Clark's drawing abilities test. In J. S. Renzulli (Ed.), *Identification of students for gifted and talented programs* (pp. 101–115). Thousand Oaks, CA: Corwin.

Clark, G., & Zimmerman, E. (1997). *Project ARTS: Programs for ethnically diverse, economically disadvantaged, high ability, visual arts students in rural communities: Identification, curriculum, evaluation.* (ERIC Document Reproduction Service No. ED419765)

Cline, S., & Schwartz, D. (1999). *Diverse populations of gifted children: Meeting their needs in the regular classroom and beyond.* Upper Saddle River, NJ: Prentice Hall.

Colangelo, N., Assouline, S., & Gross, M. (2004). *A nation deceived: How schools hold back America's brightest students* (Vol. 2). Iowa City, IA: Belin & Blank International Center for Gifted Education and Talent Development.

Coleman, L. J. (2004). Is consensus on a definition in the field possible, desirable, necessary? *Roeper Review, 27*, 10–11.

Coleman, M. R., & Gallagher, J. J. (1995). State identification policies: Gifted students from special populations. *Roeper Review, 17*, 268–275.

College Board. (1999). *Reaching the top: A report of the National Task Force on Minority High Achievement.* New York: Author.

Council for Exceptional Children. (2003). *What every special educator must know: Ethics, standards, and guidelines for special educators* (5th ed.). Arlington, VA: Author.

Council for Exceptional Children. (2005). *Professional standards on diversity.* Retrieved July 11, 2006, from www.cec.sped.org/Content/NavigationMenu/AboutCEC/Diversity/Profes sionalStandards/default.htm

Cross, T. L. (2004). Technology and the unseen world of gifted students. *Gifted Child Today, 27*(4), 14–15, 63–65.

Cross, T. L., & Coleman, L. J. (1993). The social cognition of gifted adolescents: An exploration of the stigma of giftedness paradigm. *Roeper Review, 16,* 37–40.

Cross, T., Stewart, R. A., & Coleman, L. (2003). Phenomenology and its implications for gifted studies research: Investigating the Lebenswelt of academically gifted students attending an elementary magnet school. *Journal for the Education of the Gifted, 26,* 201–220.

Csikszentmihalyi, M. (1988). Society, culture, and person: A systems view of creativity. In R. Sternberg (Ed.), *The nature of creativity: Contemporary psychological perspectives* (pp. 325–339). New York: Cambridge University Press.

Csikszentmihalyi, M. (1996). *Creativity: Flow and the psychology and discovery of invention.* New York: Harper Books.

Darling-Hammond, L., Wise, A. E., & Klein, S. P. (1999). *A license to teach. Raising standards for teaching.* San Francisco: Jossey-Bass.

Daugherty, M., White, C. S., & Manning, B. H. (1994). Relationships among private speech and creativity measurements of young children. *Gifted Child Quarterly, 38,* 21–26.

Davalos, R., & Haensly, P. (1997). After the dust has settled: Youth reflect on their high school mentored research experience. *Roeper Review, 19,* 204–207.

Delisle, J., & Galbraith, J. (2002). *When gifted kids don't have all the answers: How to meet their social and emotional needs.* Minneapolis, MN: Free Spirit.

Dettmer, P. A., & Landrum, M. S. (Eds.). (1998). *Staff development: The key to effective gifted education programs.* Waco, TX: Prufrock Press.

Dettmer, P. A., Landrum, M. S., & Miller, T. N. (2006). Professional development for the education of secondary gifted students. In F. A. Dixon & S. M. Moon (Eds.), *The handbook of secondary gifted education* (pp. 611–648). Waco, TX: Prufrock Press.

Diaz, E. I. (1998). Perceived factors influencing the academic underachievement of talented students of Puerto Rican descent. *Gifted Child Quarterly 42,* 105–122.

Dixon, F. A., Lapsley, D., & Hanchon, T. A. (2004). An empirical typology of perfectionism in gifted adolescents. *Gifted Child Quarterly. 48,* 95–106.

Elder, L., & Paul, R. (2003). *Analytic thinking: How to take thinking apart and what to look for when you do.* Dillon Beach, CA: Foundation for Critical Thinking.

Elhoweris, H., Mutua, K., Alsheikh, N., & Holloway, P. (2005). Effects of children's ethnicity on teachers' referral and recommendation decisions in gifted and talented programs. *Remedial and Special Education, 26*(1), 25–31.

Emerick, L. J. (1992). Academic underachievement among the gifted: Students' perceptions of factors that reverse the pattern. *Gifted Child Quarterly, 36,* 140–146.

Ericcson, K. A., & Charness, N. (1994). Expert performance: Its structure and acquisition. *American Psychologist, 49,* 725–747.

Feldhusen, J. F. (1996). Is it acceleration or simply appropriate instruction for precocious youth? *Teaching Exceptional Children, 28,* 48–51.

Feldhusen, J. F., Asher, J. W., & Hoover, S. M. (2004). Problems in the identification of giftedness, talent, or ability. In J. S. Renzulli (Ed.), *Identification of students for gifted and talented programs* (pp. 79–85). Thousand Oaks, CA: Corwin.

Feldhusen, J. F., & Kennedy, D. M. (1988). Preparing gifted youth for leadership roles in a rapidly changing society. *Roeper Review, 10,* 226–230.

Feldman, D. (1980). *Beyond universals in cognitive development.* Norwood, NJ: Ablex.

Fernández, A. T., Gay, L. R., Lucky, L F., & Gavilan, M. R. (1998). Teacher perceptions of gifted Hispanic limited English proficient students. *Journal for the Education of the Gifted, 21,* 335–351.

Fishman, B. J., Marx, R. W., Best, S., & Tal, R. T. (2003). Linking teacher and student learning to improve professional development in systemic reform. *Teaching and Teacher Education, 19,* 643–658.

Ford, D. (1996). *Reversing underachievement among gifted black students: Promising practices and programs.* New York: Teachers College Press.

Ford, D. Y. (2004a). A challenge for culturally diverse families of gifted children: Forced choices between affiliation or achievement. *Gifted Child Today, 27*(3), 26–29.

Ford, D. Y. (2004b). *Intelligence testing and cultural diversity: Concerns, cautions, and considerations* (Research Monograph 04204). Storrs: University of Connecticut, National Research Center on the Gifted and Talented.

Ford, D. Y., & Harris, J. J., III (1997). A study of the racial identity and achievement of Black males and females. *Roeper Review, 20,* 105–110.

Ford, D. Y., & Harris, J. J., III (1999). *Multicultural gifted education.* New York: Teachers College Press.

Ford, D. Y., & Harris, J. J., III (2000). A framework for infusing multicultural curriculum into gifted education. *Roeper Review, 23,* 4–10.

Ford, D. Y., Moore, J. L., III, & Milner, H. R. (2005). Beyond culture blindness: A model of culture with implications for gifted education. *Roeper Review, 27*(2), 97–103.

Ford, D. Y., & Thomas, A. (1997). *Underachievement among gifted minority students: problems and promise* (ERIC Digest E544). Reston, VA: ERIC Clearinghouse on Disabilities and Gifted Education.

Ford, D. Y., & Trotman, M. F. (2001). Teachers of gifted students: Suggested multicultural characteristics and competencies. *Roeper Review, 23,* 235–239.

Frasier, M. M. (1991). Disadvantaged and culturally diverse gifted students. *Journal for the Education of the Gifted, 14,* 234–245.

Frasier, M. M., Hunsaker, S. L., Lee, J., Finley, V. S., Frank, E., & Garcia, J. H. (1995). *Educators' perceptions of barriers to the identification of gifted children from economically disadvantaged and limited English proficient backgrounds* (Research Monograph 95216). Storrs: University of Connecticut, National Research Center on the Gifted and Talented.

Frey, C. P. (1998). Struggling with identity: Working with seventh-and eighth-grade gifted girls to air issues of concern. *Journal for the Education of the Gifted, 21,* 437–451.

Frey, C. P. (2000). A writer's workshop for highly verbal students. *Gifted Child Today, 23*(5), 38–43.

Gagné, F. (1985). Giftedness and talent: Reexamining a reexamination of the definitions. *Gifted Child Quarterly, 29,* 103–112.

Gagné, F. (1995). From giftedness to talent: A developmental model and its impact on the language of the field. *Roeper Review, 18,* 103–111.

Gagné, F. (2000). Understanding the complex choreography of talent development through DMGT-based analysis. In K. A. Heller, F. J. Mönks, R. Sternberg, & R. Subotnik (Eds.), *International handbook of research and development of giftedness and talent* (2nd ed., pp. 67–79). New York: Elsevier.

Gagné, F. (2003). Transforming gifts into talents: The DMGT as a developmental theory. In N. Colangelo & G. Davis (Eds.), *Handbook of gifted education* (3rd ed., pp. 60–74). New York: Pearson.

Gallagher, S. (1997). Problem-based learning: Where did it come from, what does it do, and where is it going? *Journal for the Education of the Gifted, 20,* 332–362.

Gallagher, S. A., & Stepien, W. (1996). Content acquisition in problem-based learning: Depth versus breadth in American studies. *Journal for the Education of the Gifted, 19,* 257–275.

Galton, F. (1865). Hereditary talent and character. *Macmillan's Magazine, 12,* 157–166, 318–327.

García, S. B., & Guerra, P. L. (2004). Deconstructing deficit thinking. Working with educators to create more equitable learning environments. *Education and Urban Society, 36*(2), 150–168.

Gardner, H. (1983/1994). *Frames of mind: The theory of multiple intelligences.* New York: Basic Books.

Gardner, H. (1993). *Creating minds: An anatomy of creativity seen through the lives of Fred, Einstein, Picasso, Stravinsky, Eliot, Graham, and Gandhi.* New York: Basic Books.

Garet, M. S., Porter, A. C., Desimone, L., Birman, B. F., & Yoon, K. S. (2001). What makes professional development effective? Results from a national sample of teachers. *American Educational Research Journal, 38,* 915–945.

Garrison, L. (1993). Professionals of the future: Will they be female? Will they be ethnically diverse? *Roeper Review, 15*, 161–164.

Gay, G. (2002). Preparing for culturally responsive teaching. *Journal of Teacher Education, 53*, 106–116.

Gentry, M. (1999). *Promoting student achievement and exemplary classroom practices through cluster grouping: A research-based alternative to heterogeneous elementary classrooms* (Research Monograph 9918). Storrs: University of Connecticut, National Research Center on the Gifted and Talented.

Good, C., Aronson, J., & Inzlicht, M. (2003). Improving adolescents' standardized test performance: An intervention to reduce the effects of stereotype threat. *Journal of Applied Developmental Psychology, 24*, 645–662.

Grantham, T., & Ford, D. (1998). A case study of the social needs of Danisha: An underachieving gifted African-American female. *Roeper Review, 21*, 96–101.

Grantham, T. C., & Ford, D. Y. (2003). Beyond self-concept and self esteem: Racial identity and gifted African American students. *High School Journal, 87*, 18–29.

Greene, M. (2003). Gifted adrift? Career counseling of the gifted and talented. *Roeper Review, 25*, 66–72.

Gross, M. U. M. (2002). Musings: Gifts to the gifted—training our teachers. *Understanding Our Gifted, 15*(1), 25–27.

Gross, M. (2003). *Exceptionally gifted children*. London: RoutledgeFalmer.

Grybe, D. (1997). Mentoring the gifted and talented. *Preventing School Failure, 41*, 115.

Gubbins, E. J., Westberg, K. L., Reis, S. M., Dinnocenti, S. T., Tieso, C. L., & Muller, L. M. (2002). *Implementing a professional development model using gifted education strategies with all students* (Research Monograph 02172). Storrs: University of Connecticut, National Research Center on the Gifted and Talented.

Guilford, J. P. (1967). *The nature of human intelligence*. New York: McGraw-Hill.

Guskey, T. R. (1991). Enhancing the effectiveness of professional development programs. *Journal of Educational and Psychological Consultation, 2*, 239–247.

Guskey, T. R. (2000). *Evaluating professional development*. Thousand Oaks, CA: Corwin.

Guskey, T. R. (2003a). Analyzing lists of the characteristics of effective professional development to promote visionary leadership. *National Association of Secondary School Principals (NASSP) Bulletin, 87*, 4–20.

Guskey, T. R. (2003b). What makes professional development effective? *Phi Delta Kappan, 84*, 748–750.

Guskey, T. R. (2007). Multiple sources of evidence: An analysis of stakeholders' perceptions of various indicators of student learning. *Educational Measurement: Issues and Practice, 26*(1), 19–27.

Guskey, T. R., & Sparks, D. (1991, November). What to consider when evaluating staff development. *Educational Leadership*, 73–76.

Hansen, J. B., & Feldhusen, J. F. (1994). Comparison of trained and untrained teachers of gifted students. *Gifted Child Quarterly, 38*, 115–123.

Harmon, D. (2002). They won't teach me: The voices of gifted African American inner-city students. *Roeper Review, 24*, 68–75.

Haycock, K. (2006, May 5). *Closing the achievement gap: Lessons from schools and districts on the performance frontier*. Keynote presentation, inaugural symposium of the National Center for Urban School Transformation, San Diego, CA.

Hébert, T. P. (1991). Meeting the affective needs of bright boys through bibliotherapy. *Roeper Review, 13*, 207–212.

Hébert, T. P. (1993). Reflections at graduation: The long-term impact of elementary school experiences in creative productivity. *Roeper Review, 16*, 22–28.

Hébert, T. P. (1998). Gifted Black males in an urban high school: Factors that influence achievement and underachievement. *Journal for the Education of the Gifted, 21*, 385–414.

Hébert, T. (2002). Educating gifted children from low socioeconomic backgrounds: Creating visions of a hopeful future. *Exceptionality, 10*, 127–138.

Hébert, T. P., & Neumeister, K. L. S. (2000). University mentors in the elementary classroom: Supporting the intellectual, motivational, and emotional needs of high-ability students. *Journal for the Education of the Gifted, 24,* 122–148.

Hertzog, N. B. (1998). The changing role of the gifted education specialist. *Teaching Exceptional Children, 30,* 39–43.

Hertzog, N. B. (2003). Advocacy: "On the cutting edge . . ." *Gifted Child Quarterly, 47,* 66–81.

Hertzog, N., & Bennett, T. (2004). In whose eyes? Parents' perspectives on the learning needs of their gifted children. *Roeper Review, 26,* 96–104.

Hollingworth, L. S. (1942). *Children above 180 IQ.* Yonkers, NY: World Book Company.

Hong, E, Greene, M. T., & Higgins, K. (2006). Instructional practices of teachers in general education classrooms and gifted resource rooms: Development and validation of the Instructional Practice Questionnaire. *Gifted Child Quarterly, 50,* 91–103.

Howard, B. B. (2005). *Teacher growth and assessment process: Procedural handbook.* Greensboro, NC: US Department of Education, South Eastern Regional Vision for Education. (ERIC Document Reproduction Service No. ED485231)

Huff, R. E., Houskamp, B. M., Watkins, A. V., Stanton, M., & Tavegia, B. (2005). The experiences of parents of gifted African American children: A phenomenological study. *Roeper Review, 27*(4), 215–221.

Hughes, L. (1999). Action research and practical inquiry: How can I meet the needs of the high-ability student within my regular education classroom? *Journal for the Education of the Gifted, 22,* 282–297.

Hunsaker, S. (1995). *Family influences on the achievement of economically disadvantaged students: Implications for gifted identification and programming* (Research Monograph 95206). Storrs: University of Connecticut, National Research Center on the Gifted and Talented.

Hunsaker, S. L., & Callahan, C. M. (1995). Creativity and giftedness: Published instrument uses and abuses. *Gifted Child Quarterly, 39,* 110–114.

Hyde, J. S., Fennema, E., Ryan, M., & Frost, L. A. (1990). Gender comparisons of mathematics attitudes and affect: A meta-analysis. *Psychology of Women Quarterly, 14,* 299–324.

Ingram, M. A. (2003). Sociocultural poetry to assist gifted students in developing empathy for the lived experiences of others. *Journal of Secondary Gifted Education, 14,* 83–90.

International Reading Association & National Association for the Education of Young Children. (1998). Learning to read and write: Developmentally appropriate practices for young children. *Young Children, 53*(4), 30–46.

Irvine, D. J. (1991). Gifted education without a state mandate: The importance of vigorous advocacy. *Gifted Child Quarterly, 35,* 196–199.

Johnsen, S. K. (Ed.). (2004). *Identifying gifted students: A practical guide.* Waco, TX: Prufrock Press.

Johnsen, S., & Goree, K. (2005). Teaching gifted students through independent study. In F. Karnes & S. Bean (Eds.), *Methods and materials for teaching the gifted and talented* (pp. 379–408). Waco, TX: Prufrock Press.

Johnsen, S. K., Haensly, P. A., Ryser, G. R., & Ford, R. F. (2002). Changing general education classroom practices to adapt for gifted students. *Gifted Child Quarterly, 46*(1), 45–63.

Johnsen, S. K., & Pennington, P. (2005, April). *Alternative assessments for a gifted teacher education program.* Division Showcase at the annual convention of the International Council for Exceptional Children, Salt Lake City, UT.

Johnson, D. T., Boyce, L. N., & VanTassel-Baska, J. (1995). Science curriculum review: evaluating materials for high-ability learners. *Gifted Child Quarterly, 39,* 36–45.

Johnson, N. (1994). *Understanding gifted underachievers in an ethnically diverse population.* (ERIC Document Reproduction Services No. ED368101)

Kanevsky, L., & Keighley, T. (2003). To produce or not to produce? Understanding boredom and the honor in underachievement. *Roeper Review, 26,* 20–28.

Kaplan, S. (2005). Layering differentiated curricula for the gifted and talented. In F. Karnes & S. Bean (Eds.), *Methods and materials for teaching the gifted* (pp. 107–132). Waco, TX: Prufrock Press.

Karnes, F. A., & Marquardt. R. G. (1997a). The fragmented framework of legal protection for the gifted. *Peabody Journal of Education, 72*(3&4), 166–179.

Karnes, F. A., & Marquardt, R. (1997b). *Know your legal rights in gifted education* (ERIC Digest E541). Reston, VA: ERIC Clearinghouse on Disabilities and Gifted Education.

Karnes, F. A., Meriweather, S., & D'Ilio, V. (1987). The effectiveness of the leadership studies program. *Roeper Review, 9,* 238–241.

Karnes, F. A., & Shaunessy, E. (2004). The application of an individual professional development plan to gifted education. *Gifted Child Today, 27*(3), 60–64.

Keller, J. D. (1999). Deciphering teacher lounge talk. *Phi Delta Kappan, 81*(4), 328–329.

Kennedy, M. (1999). Form and substance in mathematics and science professional development. *NISE Brief, 3*(2), 1–7.

Kerr, B., & Cohn, S. (2001). *Smart boys: Talent, manhood, and the search for meaning.* Scottsdale, AZ: Great Potential Press.

Kerr, B., & Kurpius, S. (2004). Encouraging talented girls in math and science: Effects of a guidance intervention. *High Ability Studies, 15,* 85–102.

Kerr, B., & Sodano, S. (2003). Career assessment with intellectually gifted students. *Journal of Career Assessment, 11,* 168–186.

Kingore, B. (1995). Introducing parents to portfolio assessment: A collaborative effort toward authentic assessment. *Gifted Child Today, 18*(4), 12–13, 40.

Kirschenbaum, R. J. (2004). Dynamic assessment and its use with underserved gifted and talented populations. In A. Baldwin & S. Reis (Eds.), *Culturally diverse and underserved populations of gifted students. Essential reading in gifted education* (pp. 49–62). Thousand Oaks, CA: Corwin.

Kirschenbaum, R. J., Armstrong, D. C., & Landrum, M. S. (1999). Resource consultation model in gifted education to support talent development in today's inclusive schools. *Gifted Child Quarterly, 43,* 39–47.

Kitano, M. (1997). Gifted African American women. *Journal for the Education of the Gifted, 21,* 254–287.

Kitano, M. K., & Espinosa, R. (1995). Language diversity and giftedness: Working with gifted English language learners. *Journal for the Education of the Gifted, 18,* 234–254.

Kitano, M. K., & Pedersen, K. S. (2002a). Action research and practical inquiry. Multicultural content integration in gifted education: Lessons from the field. *Journal for the Education of the Gifted, 25*(3), 269–289.

Kitano, M. K., & Pedersen, K. S. (2002b). Action research and practical inquiry: Teaching gifted English learners. *Journal for the Education of the Gifted, 26*(2), 132–147.

Kitano, M., & Perkins, C. (1996). International gifted women: Developing a critical human resource. *Roeper Review, 19,* 34–40.

Knight, S. L., & Wiseman, D. L. (2005). Professional development for teachers of diverse students: A summary of the research. *Journal of Education for Students Placed at Risk, 10*(4), 387–405.

Kolesinski, M. T., & Leroux, J. A. (1992). The bilingual education experience, French-English, Spanish-English: From a perspective of gifted students. *Roeper Review, 14,* 221–224.

Kraft, N. P. (2001, April). *Standards in teacher education: A critical analysis of NCATE, INTASC, and NBPTS.* Paper presented at annual meeting of the American Educational Research Association, Seattle, WA.

Krebs, A. S. (2005). Analyzing student work as a professional development activity. *School Science and Mathematics, 105,* 402–411.

Kulik, J. A. (1992). *An analysis of the research on ability grouping: Historical and contemporary perspectives* (RBDM9204). Storrs: University of Connecticut, National Research Center on the Gifted and Talented.

Kulik, J. A., & Kulik, C. C. (1992). Meta-analytic findings on grouping programs. *Gifted Child Quarterly, 36,* 73–77.

Kurlaender, M., & Yun, J. T. (2001). Is diversity a compelling educational interest? Evidence from Louisville. In G. Orfield (Ed.), *Diversity challenged: Evidence on the impact of affirmative action* (pp. 111–141). Cambridge, MA: Harvard Education Publishing Group.

Landau, E., & Weissler, K. (1998). The relationship between emotional maturity, intelligence and creativity in gifted children. *Gifted Education International, 13,* 100–105.

Landry, S. H., Swank, P. R., Smith, K. E., Assel, M. A., & Gunnewig, S. B. (2006). Enhancing early literacy skills for preschool children: Bringing a professional development model to scale. *Journal of Learning Disabilities, 39,* 306–324.

Landrum, M. (2001). Resource consultation and collaboration in gifted education. *Psychology in the Schools, 38,* 457–465.

Landrum, M. S. (2003). *Consultation in gifted education: Teachers working together to serve students.* Mansfield, CT: Creative Learning.

Landrum, M. S., Callahan, C. M., & Shaklee, B. D. (2001). *Aiming for excellence: Annotations to the NAGC pre-k-grade 12 gifted program standards.* Waco, TX: Prufrock Press.

Limburg-Weber, L. (1999/2000). Send them packing: Study abroad as an option for gifted students. *Journal of Secondary Gifted Education, 11,* 43–51.

Litton, E. F. (1999). Learning in America: The Filipino-American sociocultural perspective. In C. C. Park & M. M. Chi (Eds.), *Asian-American education: Prospects and challenges* (pp. 131–153). Westport, CT: Bergin & Garvey.

Louis, B., & Lewis, M. (1992). Parental beliefs about giftedness in young children and their relation to actual ability level. *Gifted Child Quarterly, 36,* 27–31.

Lovecky, D. (1995). Ramifications of giftedness for girls. *Journal of Secondary Gifted Education, 6,* 157–164.

Lupkowski-Shoplik, A. E., & Assouline, S. G. (1994). Evidence of extreme mathematical precocity: Case studies of talented youths. *Roeper Review, 16,* 144–151.

Lynch, E. W., & Hanson, M. J. (2004). *Developing cross-cultural competence* (3rd ed.). Baltimore, MD: Paul H. Brookes.

Lynch, S. J. (1992). Fast-paced high school science for the academically talented: A six-year perspective. *Gifted Child Quarterly, 36,* 147–154.

Maker, J. (1994). Authentic assessment of problem solving and giftedness in secondary school students. *Journal of Secondary Gifted Education, 6,* 19–29.

Marland, S. P. (1972). *Education of the gifted and talented: Report to the Congress of the United States by the U.S. commissioner of education.* Washington, DC: Government Printing Office.

Masten, W. G., & Plata, M. (2000). Acculturation and teacher ratings of Hispanic and Anglo-American students. *Roeper Review, 23,* 45–46.

Matthews, D. J., & Foster, J. F. (2005). A dynamic scaffolding model of teacher development: The gifted education consultant as catalyst for change. *Gifted Child Quarterly, 49,* 222–230.

Matthews, P. H., & Matthews, M. S. (2004). Heritage language instruction and giftedness in language minority students: Pathways toward success. *Journal of Secondary Gifted Education, 15,* 50–55.

McLaughlin, S. C., & Saccuzzo, D. P. (1997). Ethnic and gender differences in locus of control in children referred for gifted programs: The effects of vulnerability factors. *Journal for the Education of the Gifted, 20,* 268–284.

Melber, L. M. (2003). Partnerships in science learning: Museum outreach and elementary gifted education. *Gifted Child Quarterly, 47,* 251–258.

Mendaglio, S. (1995). Sensitivity among gifted persons: A multi-faceted perspective. *Roeper Review 17,* 69–72.

Milgram, R. M., Hong, E., Shavit, Y. W., & Peled, R. W. (1997). Out-of-school activities in gifted adolescents as a predictor of vocational choice and work accomplishment in young adults. *Journal of Secondary Gifted Education, 8,* 111–120.

Miller, L. S. (2004). *Promoting sustained growth in the representation of African Americans, Latinos, and Native Americans among top students in the United Sates at all levels of the education system* (Research Monograph 04190). Storrs: University of Connecticut, National Research Center on the Gifted and Talented.

Mills, C. J., Stork, E. J., & Krug, D. (1992). Recognition and development of academic talent in educationally disadvantaged students. *Exceptionality, 3,* 165–180.

Milne, H., & Reis, S. (2000). Using video therapy to address the social and emotional needs of gifted children. *Gifted Child Today, 23*(1), 24–29.

Milner, H. R., & Ford, D. Y. (2005). Racial experiences influence us as teachers: Implications for gifted education curriculum development and implementation. *Roeper Review, 28*(1), 30–36.

Miserandino, A. D., Subotnik, R. F., & Ou, K. (1995). Identifying and nurturing mathematical talent in urban school settings. *Journal of Secondary Gifted Education, 6*, 245–257.

Moon, S. (Ed.). (2004). *Social/Emotional issues, underachievement, counseling of gifted and talented students.* Thousand Oaks, CA: Corwin.

Moon, S. M., Feldhusen, J. F., & Dillon, D. R. (1994). Long-term effect of an enrichment program based on the Purdue Three-Stage Model. *Gifted Child Quarterly, 38*, 38–48.

Moon, S. M., Jurich, J. A., & Feldhusen, J. F. (1998). Families of gifted children: Cradles of development. In R. C. Friedman & K. Rogers (Eds.), *Talent in context: Historical and social perspectives on giftedness* (pp. 81–99). Washington, DC: American Psychological Association.

Moon, T. R., & Callahan, C. M. (2001). Curricular modifications, family outreach, and a mentoring program. *Journal for the Education of the Gifted, 24*, 305–321.

Montgomery, D., Otto, S., & Hull, D. (2007). *Project CREATES: Connecting community resources encouraging all teachers to educate with spirit: Research report for learning in the arts.* Stillwater: Oklahoma State University.

Morehead, M. A. (1998). Professional behaviors for the beginning teacher. *American Secondary Education, 26*(4), 22–26.

Morissette, N. B. (2006). *Parent participation programs: Examining the needs of parents of gifted minority students.* Unpublished master's project, McGill University.

Myers, W. A. (1993/1994). Two plus two does not always equal four (years). *Journal of Secondary Gifted Education, 5*(2), 27–30.

National Association for Gifted Children and the Council of State Directors of Programs for the Gifted. (2005). *2004–2005 State of the states: A report by the National Association for Gifted Children and the Council of State Directors of Programs.* Washington, DC: Author.

National Association for Gifted Children. (2006). *The big picture.* Retrieved July 4, 2006, from www.nagc.org/CMS400Min/index.aspx?id=532

National Council for Accreditation of Teacher Education. (2006). *Professional standards for the accreditation of schools, colleges, and departments of education.* Retrieved March 19, 2007, from www.ncate.org

Neihart, M. (1999). The impact of giftedness on psychological well-being: What does the empirical literature say? *Roeper Review, 22*, 10–17.

Norton, D. E., & Norton, S. (2002). *Through the eyes of a child: An introduction to children's literature* (6th ed.). Upper Saddle River, NJ: Prentice Hall.

Noyce, P. (2006). Professional development: How do we know if it works? *Education Week, 26*(3), 36–37, 44.

Nugent, S. A. (2005). Affective education: Addressing the social and emotional needs of gifted students in the classroom. In F. Karnes & S. Bean (Eds.), *Methods and materials for teaching the gifted* (2nd ed., pp. 409–438). Waco, TX: Prufrock Press.

Ogbu, J. U. (1994). Understanding cultural diversity and learning. *Journal for the Education of the Gifted, 17*, 355–383.

Ogbu, J. (1995). Understanding cultural diversity and learning. In J. A. Banks & C. A. McGee (Eds.), *Handbook of research on multicultural education* (pp. 582–583). New York: Macmillan. (ERIC Document Reproduction Services No. ED382727)

Olszewski-Kubilius, P. (1998). Early entrance to college: Students' stories. *Journal of Secondary Gifted Education, 10*, 226–247.

Olszewski-Kubilius, P., & Lee, S. (2004). Parent perceptions of effects of the Saturday Enrichment Program on gifted students' talent development. *Roeper Review, 26*, 156–165.

Oreck, B. A, Owen, S. V., & Baum, S. M. (2003). Validity, reliability, and equity issues in an observational talent assessment process in the performing arts. *Journal for the Education of the Gifted, 27*, 62–94.

Parker, J. (1996). NAGC standards for personnel preparation in gifted education: A brief history. *Gifted Child Quarterly, 40,* 158–164.

Parker, J. P., & Begnaud, L. G. (2003). *Developing creative leadership.* Gifted Treasury Series. Portsmouth, NH: Teacher Ideas Press.

Parrett, W. H. (2005). Against all odds: Reversing low achievement of one school's Native American Students. *School Administrator, 62*(1), 26–29.

Passow, A. H., & Frasier, M. M. (1994). Toward improving identification of talent potential among minority and disadvantaged students. *Roeper Review, 18,* 198–202.

Pearl, P. (1997). Why some parent education programs for parents of gifted children succeed and others do not. *Early Child Development and Care, 130,* 41–48.

Pedersen, K. S., & Kitano, M. K. (2006). Designing a multicultural literature unit for gifted learners. *Gifted Child Today, 29*(2), 38–49.

Perry, T., Steele, C., & Hilliard, A. (2003). *Young, gifted and Black. Promoting high achievement among African-American students.* Boston: Beacon Press.

Peterson, J. S. (2003). An argument for proactive attention to affective concerns of gifted adolescents. *Journal of Secondary Gifted Education, 14,* 62–71.

Peterson, J. S., & Margolin, L. (1997). Naming gifted children: An example of unintended "reproduction." *Journal for the Education of the Gifted, 21,* 82–101.

Peterson, J. S., & Rischar, H. (2000). Gifted and gay: A study of the adolescent experience. *Gifted Child Quarterly, 44,* 231–246.

Piechowski, M. M. (1992). Giftedness for all seasons: Inner peace in time of war. In N. Colangelo, S. G. Assouline, & D. I. Ambroson (Eds.), *Talent development. Proceedings from the 1991 Henry B. & Jocelyn Wallace National Research Symposium on Talent Development* (pp. 180–203). Unionville, NY: Trillium Press.

Piirto, J. (1998). Themes in the lives of successful contemporary U.S. women creative writers. *Roeper Review, 21,* 60–70.

Pleiss, M. K., & Feldhusen, J. F. (1995). Mentors, role models and heroes in the lives of gifted children. *Educational Psychologist, 30,* 159–169.

Pletan, M. D., Robinson, N. M., Berninger, V. W., & Abbot, R. D. (1995). Parents' observations of kindergartners who are advanced in mathematical reasoning. *Journal for the Education of the Gifted, 19,* 30–44.

Poelzer, G. H., & Feldhusen, J. F. (1997). The international baccalaureate: A program for gifted secondary students. *Roeper Review, 19,* 168–171.

Professional Standards and Practices Standing Committee. (2003, June). *Language defining the knowledge bases for the knowledge and skills.* (Available from the Professional Standards and Practices Committee, Council for Exceptional Children, 1110 North Glebe Road, Suite 300, Arlington, VA 22201)

Public Education Network. (2005). *Teacher professional development: A primer for parents and community members.* Washington DC: Finance Project. (ERIC Document Reproduction Service No. ED484815)

Rash, P. K. (1998). Meeting parents' needs. *Gifted Child Today, 21*(5), 14–17.

Ravaglia, R., Suppes, P., Stillinger, C., & Alper, T. M. (1995). Computer-based mathematics and physics for gifted students. *Gifted Child Quarterly, 39,* 7–13.

Reid, C., Romanoff, B., Algozzine, B., & Udall, A. (2000). An evaluation of alternative screening procedures. *Journal for the Education of the Gifted, 23,* 378–396.

Reilly, J. M., & Welch, D. B. (1994/1995). Mentoring gifted young women. *Journal of Secondary Gifted Education, 6,* 120–128.

Reis, S. M., Burns, D. E., & Renzulli, J. S. (1992). *Curriculum compacting: The complete guide to modifying the regular curriculum for high ability students.* Mansfield Center, CT: Creative Learning Press.

Reis, S. M., & Renzulli, J. S. (1991). The assessment of creative products in programs for the gifted and talented. *Gifted Child Quarterly, 35*(3), 128–134.

Renzulli, J. (1994). *Schools for talent development.* Mansfield Center, CT: Creative Learning Press.

Renzulli, J. S. (2002). Emerging conceptions of giftedness: Building a bridge to the new century. *Exceptionality, 10*(2), 67–75.

Renzulli, J. S., Leppien, J. H., & Hays, T. S. (2000). *The multiple menu model: A practical guide for developing differentiated curriculum.* Mansfield Center, CT: Creative Learning Press.

Renzulli, J., & Park, S. (2002). *Giftedness and high school dropouts: Personal, family, and school related factors* (Research Monograph 02168). Storrs: University of Connecticut, National Research Center on the Gifted and Talented.

Renzulli, J. S., & Reis, S. M. (2003). The schoolwide enrichment model: Developing creative and productive giftedness. In N. Colangelo & G. A. Davis (Eds.), *Handbook of gifted education* (3rd ed., pp. 184–203*)*. Boston: Allyn & Bacon.

Renzulli, J. S., & Reis, S. M. (2004). Curriculum compacting: A research-based differentiation strategy for culturally diverse talented students. In D. Boothe & J. C. Stanley (Eds.), *In the eyes of the beholder: Critical issues for diversity in gifted education* (pp. 87–100). Waco, TX: Prufrock Press.

Reyes, E. I., Fletcher, R., & Paez, D. (1996). Developing local multidimensional screening procedures for identifying giftedness among Mexican American border populations. *Roeper Review, 18*, 208–211.

Ridges, J. (2000). Advocate role in developing district policy for gifted students. *Roeper Review, 22*, 199–201.

Riley, T. L. (1999). Put on your dancing shoes! Choreographing positive partnerships with parents of gifted children. *Gifted Child Today, 22*(4), 50–53.

Riley, T., & Karnes, F. (1998). Demonstrating creativity in the arts through competitions. *Journal of Secondary Gifted Education, 10*, 248–251.

Roberts, S. M., & Lovett, S. B. (1994). Examining the "F" in gifted: Academically gifted adolescents' physiological and affective responses to scholastic failure. *Journal for the Education of the Gifted, 17*, 241–259.

Robinson, A., & Clinkenbeard, P. R. (1998). Giftedness: An exceptionality examined. *Annual Review of Psychology, 49*, 117–139.

Robinson, A., & Kolloff, P. B. (2006). Preparing teachers to work with high-ability youth at the secondary level: Issues and implications for licensure. In F. A. Dixon & S. M. Moon (Eds.), *The handbook of secondary gifted education* (pp. 581–610). Waco, TX: Prufrock Press.

Rogers, J. A. (1998). Refocusing the lens: Using observation to assess and identify gifted learners. *Gifted Education International, 12*, 129–144.

Rogers, K. B. (1991). *The relationship of grouping practices to the education of the gifted and talented learner: Research-based decision making series.* Storrs: University of Connecticut, National Research Center on the Gifted and Talented.

Rogers, K. (2002). *Re-forming gifted education: Matching the program to the child.* Scottsdale, AZ: Great Potential Press.

Ross, P. O. (1991). Advocacy for gifted programs in the new educational climate. *Gifted Child Quarterly, 35*, 173–176.

Rossett, A., & Sheldon, K. (2001). *Beyond the podium: Delivering training and performance to a digital world.* San Francisco: Jossey-Bass.

Rotigel, J., & Lupkowski-Shoplik, A. (1999). Using talent searches to identify and meet the educational needs of mathematically talented youngsters. *School Science and Mathematics, 99*, 330.

Rowley, S. J., & Moore, J. A. (2002). Racial identity in context for the gifted African American student. *Roeper Review, 24*, 63–67.

Schiever, S. (1991). *A comprehensive approach to teaching thinking.* Boston: Allyn & Bacon.

Schlichter, C. L., & Palmer, W. R. (Eds.). (1993). *Thinking smart: A premiere of the Talents Unlimited model.* Mansfield Center, CT: Creative Learning Press.

Schniedewind, N. (2005). "There ain't no White people here!": The transforming impact of teachers' racial consciousness on students and schools. *Equity & Excellence in Education, 38*(4), 280–289.

Schuler, P. A. (2000). Perfectionism and gifted adolescents. *Journal of Secondary Gifted Education, 11*(4), 183–196.

Shade, B. J. (Ed.). (1997). *Culture, style, and the educative process: Making schools work for racially diverse students* (2nd ed.). Springfield, IL: Charles C Thomas.

Shade, B. J., Kelly, C., & Oberg, M. (1997). *Creating culturally responsive classrooms.* Washington DC: American Psychological Association.

Shaklee, B. D., Padak, N. D., Barton, L. E., & Johnson, H. A. (1991). Educational partnerships: Gifted program advocacy in action. *Gifted Child Quarterly, 35,* 200–203.

Sharma, T. (1986). Inservicing the teachers: A pastoral tale with a moral. *Communicator, 16*(3), 4.

Siegle, D. (2002). Creating a living portfolio: Documenting student growth with electronic portfolios. *Gifted Child Today, 25*(3), 60–65.

Siegle, D. (2004). *Using media and technology with gifted learners.* Waco, TX: Prufrock Press.

Siegle, D., & McCoach, D. B. (2005). Extending learning through mentorships. In F. Karnes & S. Bean (Eds.), *Methods and materials for teaching gifted* (2nd ed., pp. 473–518). Waco, TX: Prufrock Press.

Silverman, L. K. (1997). The construct of asynchronous development. *Peabody Journal of Education, 72*(3&4), 36–58.

Solow, R. E. (1995). Parents' reasoning about the social and emotional development of their intellectually gifted children. *Roeper Review, 18,* 142–146.

Southern, W. T., & Jones, E. D. (1991). *The academic acceleration of gifted children.* New York: Teachers College Press.

Steele, C. M. (1997). A threat in the air: How stereotypes shape intellectual identity and performance. *American Psychologist, 52,* 613–629.

Stephens, K. R. (1999). Parents of the gifted and talented: The forgotten partner. *Gifted Child Today, 22*(5), 38–43, 52.

Stephens, K. R., & Karnes, F. A. (2000). State definitions for the gifted and talented revisited. *Exceptional Children, 66,* 219–238.

Sternberg, R. J. (1985). *Beyond IQ: A triarchic theory of human intelligence.* New York: Cambridge University Press.

Sternberg, R. J. (2000). Giftedness as developing expertise. In K. A. Heller, F. J. Mönks, R. J. Sternberg, & R. F. Subotnik (Eds.), *International handbook of research and development of giftedness and talent* (2nd ed., pp. 55–66). New York: Elsevier.

Sternberg, R. J., Torff, B., & Grigorenko, E. L. (1998). Teaching triarchically improves school achievement. *Journal of Educational Psychology, 90,* 374–384.

Stichter, J. P., Lewis, T. J., Richter, J., Johnson, N. W., & Bradley, L. (2006). Assessing antecedent variables: The effects of instructional variables on student outcomes through in-service and peer coaching professional development models. *Education and Treatment of Children, 29,* 665–692.

Stormont, M., Stebbins, M. S., & Holliday, G. (2001). Characteristics and educational support needs of underrepresented gifted adolescents. *Psychology in the Schools, 38,* 413–423.

Strip, C., & Hirsch, G. (2001). Trust and teamwork: The parent-teacher partnership for helping the gifted child. *Gifted Child Today, 24*(2), 26–30, 64.

Terman, L. M. (1925). *Genetic studies of genius.* Palo Alto, CA: Stanford University Press.

Terry, A. W. (2003). Effects of service learning on young, gifted adolescents and their community. *Gifted Child Quarterly, 47,* 295–308.

Thompson, M. C., & Thompson, M. B. (1996). Reflection on foreign language study for highly able learners. In J. VanTassel-Baska, D. T. Johnson, & L. N. Boyce (Eds.), *Developing verbal talent: Ideas and strategies for teachers of elementary and middle school students* (pp. 174–188). Boston: Allyn & Bacon.

Tomlinson, C. A. (2001). *How to differentiate instruction in mixed ability classrooms* (2nd ed.). Alexandria, VA: Association for Supervision and Curriculum Development.

Tomlinson, C. A. (2002). Different learners, different lessons. *Instructor, 112*(2), 21, 24–26 SLW.

Tomlinson, C. A., & Cunningham-Eidson, C. (2003). *Differentiation in practice: A resource guide for differentiating curriculum, grades K–5.* Alexandria, VA: Association for Supervision and Curriculum Development.

Tomlinson, C. A., Kaplan, S. N., Renzulli, J., Burns, D. E., Leppien, J. H., & Purcell, J. H. (2001). *The parallel curriculum: A model for planning curriculum for gifted students and whole classrooms.* Thousand Oaks, CA: Corwin.

Torrance, E. P. (1962). *Guiding creative talent.* Englewood Cliffs, NJ: Prentice Hall.

Torrance, E. P. (1984). *Mentor relationships: How they aid creative achievement, endure, change and die.* Buffalo, NY: Bearly Limited.

Treffinger, D. (1994). Productive thinking: Toward authentic instruction and assessment. *Journal of Secondary Gifted Education, 6,* 30–37.

Tyler-Wood, T., & Carri, L. (1993). Verbal measures of cognitive ability: The gifted low SES student's albatross. *Roeper Review, 16,* 102–105.

Uresti, R., Goertz, J., & Bernal, E. M. (2002). Maximizing achievement for potentially gifted and talented and regular minority students in a primary classroom. *Roeper Review, 25,* 27–31.

U.S. Department of Education. (1993). *National excellence: A case for developing America's talent.* Washington, DC: Government Printing Office.

U.S. Office of Civil Rights. (2004). *Civil rights data collection: 2004.* Retrieved June 1, 2007, from http://vistademo.beyond2020.com/ocr2004rv30/wdsdata.html

Valdes, G. (2002). *Understanding the special giftedness of young interpreters* (Research Monograph 02158). Storrs: University of Connecticut, National Research Center on the Gifted and Talented.

van Stekelenburg, A. V. (1984). *Classics for the gifted: Evaluation.* South Africa: Retrieved March 18, 2005, from ERIC database.

VanTassel-Baska, J. (1982). Results of a Latin-based experimental study of the verbally precocious. *Roeper Review, 4,* 35–37.

VanTassel-Baska, J. (1992). *Planning effective curriculum for gifted learners.* Denver, CO: Love.

VanTassel-Baska, J. (1998). The development of academic talent. *Phi Delta Kappan, 79,* 760–763.

VanTassel-Baska, J. (2002). Assessment of gifted student learning in the language arts. *Journal of Secondary Gifted Education, 13,* 67–72.

VanTassel-Baska, J. (2003a). Content-based curriculum for high-ability learners: An introduction. In J. VanTassel-Baska & C. A. Little (Eds.), *Content-based curriculum for high-ability learners* (pp. 1–23). Waco, TX: Prufrock Press.

VanTassel-Baska, J. (2003b). *Content-based curriculum for low income and minority gifted learners* (Research Monograph 03180). Storrs: University of Connecticut, National Research Center on the Gifted and Talented.

VanTassel-Baska, J. (2003c). *Differentiating the language arts for high ability learners, K–8* (ERIC Digest E640). Arlington, VA: ERIC Clearinghouse on Disabilities and Gifted Education. Retrieved March 25, 2005, from ERIC database.

VanTassel-Baska, J. (2003d). Implementing innovative curricular and instructional practices in classrooms and schools. In J. VanTassel-Baska & C. A. Little (Eds.), *Content-based curriculum for high-ability learners* (pp. 355–375). Waco, TX: Prufrock Press.

VanTassel-Baska, J. (2004). Metaevaluation findings: A call for gifted program quality. In J. VanTassel-Baska & A. X. Feng (Eds.), *Designing and utilizing evaluation for gifted program improvement* (pp. 227–245). Waco, TX: Prufrock Press.

VanTassel-Baska, J., Avery, L. D., Little, C., & Hughes, C. (2000). An evaluation of the implementation of curriculum innovation: The impact of the William and Mary units on schools. *Journal for the Education of the Gifted, 23,* 244–272.

VanTassel-Baska, J., Avery, L., Struck, J., Feng, A., Bracken, B., Drummond, D., & Stambaugh, T. (2003). *The William and Mary classroom observation scales* (Rev.). Williamsburg, VA: College of William and Mary, School of Education, Center for Gifted Education. (Funded by the Jacob Javits Grant, U.S. Department of Education)

VanTassel-Baska, J., Johnson, D., & Avery, L. D. (2002). Using performance tasks in the identification of economically disadvantaged and minority gifted learners: Findings from Project STAR. *Gifted Child Quarterly, 46,* 110–123.

VanTassel-Baska, J., Johnson, D. T., Hughes, C. E., & Boyce, L. N. (1996). A study of language arts curriculum effectiveness with gifted learners. *Journal for the Education of the Gifted, 19,* 461–480.

VanTassel-Baska, J., & Little, C. A. (Eds.). (2003). *Content-based curriculum for gifted learners.* Waco, TX: Prufrock Press.

VanTassel-Baska, J., Olszewski-Kubilius, P., & Kulieke, M. (1994). A study of self-concept and social support in advantaged and disadvantaged seventh and eighth grade gifted students. *Roeper Review, 16,* 186–191.

VanTassel-Baska, J., Quek, C., & Feng, A. X. (2007). The development and use of a structured teacher observation scale to assess differentiated best practice. *Roeper Review, 29,* 84–92.

VanTassel-Baska, J., & Stambaugh, T. (2006a). *Comprehensive curriculum for gifted learners* (3rd ed.). Boston: Allyn & Bacon.

VanTassel-Baska, J., & Stambaugh, T. (2006b). Project Athena: A pathway to advanced literacy development for children of poverty. *Gifted Child Today, 29*(2), 58–63.

VanTassel-Baska, J., Zuo, L., Avery, L. D., & Little, C. A. (2002). Curriculum study of gifted-student learning in the language arts. *Gifted Child Quarterly, 46,* 30–44.

Wenglinsky, H. (2000). *How teaching matters.* Princeton, NJ: Educational Testing Service.

Westberg, K., Archambault, F., Dobyns, S., & Slavin, T. (1993). *An observational study of instructional and curricular practices used with gifted and talented students in regular classrooms* (Research Monograph 93104). Storrs: University of Connecticut, National Research Center on the Gifted and Talented.

Westberg, K., & Daoust, L. (2003, Fall). The results of the replication of the Classroom Practices Survey Replication in two states. *National Research Center on the Gifted and Talented Newsletter,* pp. 3–10.

Wills, J. S., Lintz, A., & Mehan, H. (2004). Ethnographic studies of multicultural education in U.S. classrooms and schools. In J. A. Banks & C. A. M. Banks (Eds.), *Handbook of research on multicultural education* (2nd ed., pp. 163–183). San Francisco: Jossey-Bass.

Winebrenner, S. (1994). *Teaching gifted kids in the regular classroom: Strategies and techniques.* Minneapolis: Free Spirit.

Winebrenner, S. (2003). *Teaching gifted kids in the regular classroom* (2nd ed.). Minneapolis, MN: Free Spirit.

Winner, E., & Martino, G. (2000). Giftedness in non-academic domains: The case of the visual arts and music. In K. A. Heller, F. J. Mönks, R. Sternberg, & R. Subotnik (Eds.), *International handbook of research and development of giftedness and talent* (2nd ed., pp. 95–110). New York: Elsevier

Yinger, R. (1999). The role of standards in teaching and teacher education. In G. Griffin (Ed.), *The education of teachers: The 98th yearbook of the NSSE* (pp. 85–113). Chicago: University of Chicago Press.

Zamora-Duran, G., & Reyes, E. I. (1997). From tests to talking in the classroom: Assessing communicative competence. In A. J. Artiles & G. Zamora-Duran (Eds.), *Reducing disproportionate representation of culturally diverse students in special and gifted education* (pp. 47–58). Reston, VA: Council for Exceptional Children.

Index

CORWIN PRESS

The Corwin Press logo—a raven striding across an open book—represents the union of courage and learning. Corwin Press is committed to improving education for all learners by publishing books and other professional development resources for those serving the field of PreK–12 education. By providing practical, hands-on materials, Corwin Press continues to carry out the promise of its motto: **"Helping Educators Do Their Work Better."**

NATIONAL ASSOCIATION FOR
Gifted Children

Council for
Exceptional
Children

tag
The Association for the Gifted